A Garden Lover's Martha's Vineyard

A GARDEN LOVER'S
MARTHA'S VINEYARD

Text and Photographs by C . L . FORNARI

COMMONWEALTH EDITIONS

Beverly, Massachusetts

Library of Congress Cataloging-in-Publication Data

Fornari, C.L. (Cynthia Lynn), 1950–
A garden lover's Martha's Vineyard / text and photographs
by C.L. Fornari.
p. cm.
Includes index.
ISBN 978-1-933212-59-3 (alk. paper)
1. Gardens—Massachusetts—Martha's Vineyard. 2. Gardens—
Massachusetts—Martha's Vineyard—Pictorial works. I. Title.

SB466.U7M374 2008
635.09744′94—dc22   2008000093

Cover design by John Barnett / 4 Eyes Design
Interior design by Gary G. Gore
Printed in China

Published by Commonwealth Editions, an imprint of Memoirs Unlimited, Inc.,
266 Cabot Street, Beverly, Massachusetts 01915.

Visit our Web site: www.commonwealtheditions.com.

Visit C.L. Fornari on the Web at www.gardenlady.com.

This book is dedicated to those who work
to preserve the wild and the agricultural lands on Martha's Vineyard
and
to my brother, Richard Allen Albertson. We miss you.

CONTENTS

ACKNOWLEDGMENTS

I would like to thank everyone who was willing to have his or her garden photographed for *A Garden Lover's Martha's Vineyard*. You are all as generous as your gardens are beautiful. My gratitude also goes to those who were willing to take the time to share their experiences, thoughts, and expertise, for your voices add richness and veracity to this book.

Love and thanks to my husband, Dan, who supplied helpful ideas and feedback throughout and was patient with my constant need to catch early-morning ferries during an already stressful summer. Thanks to my son, Simon, for loaning me his car: leaving it in the Tisbury lot, and using the efficient Park and Ride bus service provided by the Martha's Vineyard Transit Authority, made it possible to go on and off the island frequently and easily.

Frances Tenenbaum, Susan Silva, Tom Nemmers, Thomas Mullins, Judy Jahries, Abigail Higgins, Jamie Austin, Cia Elkin, Lisina Hoch, Dee Dice, and Michael and Janice Donaroma all went out of their way to supply me with names of gardeners or locations to photograph, and I am exceedingly appreciative. I thank the members of the Martha's Vineyard Garden Club, who have been so supportive, and Tim Silva for lending me a spring parking spot near the ferry. Celeste Stickney kept me posted about what was in bloom in Edgartown, and her husband, Norman Stickney, kindly supplied an indispensable MV phone directory.

Tim Boland, Tom Clark, and Laura Coit provided information regarding Polly Hill Arboretum, and Don Sibley spoke to me at length about Mytoi; I thank them for this and for all that they do for these two marvelous island gardens.

I'm so very grateful to several garden professionals: Jeff Verner, Carly Look, Alicia Lesnikowska, and Michael Faraca. They took time from their busy schedules to show

me some stunning gardens, and much of this book's beauty comes from their talent and generosity.

And finally, my continued thanks to Ann Twombly, Webster Bull, and all of the staff at Commonwealth Editions: it is a pleasure to work with such accomplished and caring people.

INTRODUCTION

When I decided to write *A Garden Lover's Martha's Vineyard* and started traveling to the island, I expected to find the usual mix of gardens and gardeners. I knew I'd meet confirmed dirt-diggers, plant nuts, weekend gardeners, and professional landscapers. I expected to enjoy the two public gardens, Polly Hill Arboretum, in West Tisbury, and Mytoi, on Chappaquiddick, and I figured that I would photograph cut-flower sellers at the farmers' market. My expectation was that what a garden lover would like on the Vineyard was pretty similar to what would be attractive almost anywhere in the Northeast. I was right and I was wrong.

As I traveled the island from May through September, I met home vegetable gardeners who joyously grow most of the food that goes on their tables. I saw gardens made by avid plant collectors and those who love native plants. I was welcomed by professionals who garden for the love of plants and to make a living. I visited new gardeners who are beginning their relationship with plants, garden designers, plant breeders, and people with horticultural dreams.

But there was more. Over the months that I went to the island on a weekly basis, I was struck not only by the beautiful gardens I visited, but by many islanders' commitment to preserving wild spaces and local agriculture. Residents and visitors alike value the island's rich and diverse native habitats, and many work passionately to preserve them. I also met people who avidly and thoughtfully work to ensure that as much of their food as possible is island grown.

In addition to appreciating food from local sources and indigenous plant communities, scores of islanders cherish their yards and gardens. Although I think that this book reflects the wide variety of gardening on the Vineyard, it would take several volumes to include every landscape, each farm stand, all horticultural businesses, and all those who tend to island plants. For a garden lover, Martha's Vineyard is filled with riches, and it was my pleasure to discover and document a portion of this beautiful abundance.

Writing a book like this one is similar to creating a garden. After envisioning the project, you have to be willing to put in the effort needed to create what you have imagined. In the garden this means digging, hauling, and planting, and for this book it meant phoning strangers, repeated ferry trips, and visits to island properties. And whether you're creating a garden or a book, it's a given that some of what you originally pictured won't grow well, while other things will succeed well beyond your original imaginings.

In fact, gardeners with all but the most formal landscapes find that at some point the garden takes on a life of its own, and this book developed organically as well. A talk with one gardener would lead to names and phone numbers of others, and most people I approached were willing to share their properties with me and with those who read this book. In this manner I traveled from garden to garden taking photos and speaking with the gardeners, and the book grew from these visits and conversations.

The order of the book developed in much the same way. As I learned about the types of gardens on the island, heard about common challenges, and visited with gardeners, the way that the book should be organized seemed to present itself naturally.

It is not surprising that those who summered on Martha's Vineyard during childhood often return to the island when they retire. As the local inhabitants, repeat visitors, and seasonal residents might say, the beauty of the Vineyard, and the feeling that it has the best of small-town America and yet is a place apart from the norm, tends to take root in your heart. So planting colorful flowers, designing gardens, cultivating island-grown food, and working to preserve native habitats are, perhaps, all a natural response to this lovely and exceptional island.

Chapter 1

GARDENS LARGE AND SMALL

Joyful gardeners and delightful gardens abound on Martha's Vineyard, but it isn't necessarily an easy place to garden. Cold off-ocean winds delay spring planting, and the soil is—well, often far from soil. But living on the island seems to encourage an interest in the pleasures of the outdoors, including gardening. Perhaps being bounded on all sides by something as beautiful as the sea heightens the aesthetic senses. Or maybe it's that the Vineyard has a pleasing combination of wild habitat, pastoral splendor, cooling breezes, and the magnificence of the ocean, all nicely packaged within about a hundred square miles. Whatever prompts this interest, many types of gardens flourish on the island.

One Size *Doesn't* Fit All

There is tremendous interest in plants of all sorts here, and the gardens are many and varied. From small container plantings on a deck to native grasslands to several acres of formal, manicured landscapes, Martha's Vineyard has them all.

The type of garden that a homeowner chooses can be determined by location, the house's style of architecture, or the space available. Some gardens develop because of the homeowner's abilities, budget, or aesthetic preferences. Conditions on the property itself play a role: a shady site does not lend itself to an English-style perennial border, and an abundance of moist soil means that a garden of succulents might be impossible to grow. Steep hillsides, an extremely rocky terrain, or a yard composed of pure sand can dictate what type of plantings should be placed in a landscape.

Two varieties of foxgloves, *Digitalis purpurea* and the yellow *D. lutea*, mix beautifully with pink coralbells, a short dianthus, and *Nepeta* 'Six Hills Giant' in Bob and Judy Jahries' cottage-style perennial garden.

▲ Annuals and perennials make a colorful June display in the Donaromas' yard in Edgartown. The lavender *Scaevola* that's planted in the front of the beds is one of the easiest annuals available.

▶ 'New Dawn' roses cover the entire wall of the Donaromas' guesthouse in Edgartown. The 'New Dawn' climber is well loved for the pale pink flowers and the plant's overall vigor.

Those who live in a sandbox or under the shade of oak trees are not at the complete mercy of their environment, however. In some instances soil can be amended, terrain changed, or trees judiciously pruned to provide a bit more light. Gardeners are nothing if not adaptable, and it can be argued that those who live on an island are even more so.

There are times, however, when the conditions that exist are at such odds with a gardener's vision that compromises must be made. Sometimes the homeowners decide that their sand dune would be best planted with American beach grass (*Ammophila breviligulata*) instead of hydrangeas,

▲ During August the Donaromas' raised beds are filled with *Rudbeckia hirta*, nasturtiums, and other flowering annuals.

◀◀ Once the 'New Dawn' roses stop blooming, the summer annuals and perennials steal the show in the Donaromas' driveway island planting.

◀ In the early summer Michael and Janice Donaroma's raised beds are filled with assorted annuals, including the self-seeding *Silene armeria* and *Rudbeckia hirta*. The Donaromas say that the beds used to be filled with vegetables but are now planted with salad greens, flowers, and herbs.

▲▲ It is the mix of formal hedges and sheared shrubs, along with less formal plantings and a variety of foliage textures and colors, that gives Nina Schneider's gardens lasting appeal. In the period before her death, she had Zada Clark's help in maintaining the gardens.

▲ Roses and lavender flowers blend well with the silver foliage of lamb's ears in Nina Schneider's West Tisbury garden.

▲ Honeysuckle covers the arbor at the entrance to the Schneiders' garden. Over the years Nina Schneider, who was the author of many books, shared her beautiful property, and many walked with pleasure down paths through her skillfully planted gardens.

▲ Nina and Herman Schneider designed and planted a large and delightful garden on the Tiasquam River in West Tisbury. Rustic wooden arbors and ornaments and furniture collected in their travels are perfectly placed to complement the plantings.

▶ Carly Look designed casual plantings of grasses and *Vitex* around the outdoor shower at Mary Pat Thornton and Cormac McEnery's home.

for example, or a dry slope with drought-tolerant bearberry (*Arctostaphylos uva-ursi*) and switchgrass (*Panicum virgatum*).

Limited space, time, or physical capabilities might determine that a small garden is the best option. In this case, it makes sense to locate the plantings where they are easily tended and will be seen most frequently. Though in the past flower and vegetable gardens were commonly found in backyards, and lawn and foundation plants in the front, lately there has been a movement to place gardens wherever it is most practical or desirable. Perennial gardens by the

▲ Because the owner of this Edgartown garden is an artist, the well-placed stones, sculptures, and large vessels complement gardens that are planted and maintained by Donaroma's Nursery and Landscaping.

▲▶ Even on a foggy day, this wisteria-covered arbor is a delightful shady retreat.

▲ Steve Yaffee of Crosswater Landscapes planted a low-maintenance mix of grasses, perennials, and shrubs around Rick and Roberta Gross's home. Catching the light on an August afternoon are Russian sage (*Perovskia atriplicifolia*), butterfly bush (*Buddleia davidii*), *Rosa rugosa*, maiden grass (*Miscanthus sinensis*), and fountain grass (*Pennisetum alopecuroides*).

front door, vegetables along the road, or flowerbeds throughout the property are becoming the norm, and Martha's Vineyard properties are no exception.

Elizabeth Luce has a jewel box of a garden on the slope near her driveway, so the plantings can be enjoyed from the road or every time someone comes to her house. This entry garden, primarily a mix of shrubs and perennials, changes throughout the season as different plants come into bloom. It is also visible from her deck, which Elizabeth has filled with potted annuals and houseplants.

▲ An espaliered blue atlas cedar, *Cedrus atlantica* 'Glauca', fills one wall of Trudy Taylor's garden in Chilmark. Trudy has been a gardener for many years in several locations, and her love of plants and this Vineyard garden is unmistakable.

▲▶ Summer phlox, yarrow, and spirea are combined with other plants in a Chilmark border designed by Carly Look. Cups on the four corners of the table in the foreground are planted with drought-tolerant sedums.

▶ A wisely sited wisteria arbor keeps this aggressive vine away from the house in the Suhlers' garden in Edgartown. The arched arbor to the rear is covered with the pale pink flowers of 'New Dawn' roses in June.

▲ Surrounded by a fence to deter hungry rabbits, spires of blue and white delphiniums and fluffy yellow *Thalictrum flavum* bloom in Trudy Taylor's garden. Like most gardeners in the Northeast, Trudy can't depend on the delphiniums to make it through the winter, so she plants them every year as annuals.

▶ A pink spirea and groups of Asiatic lilies, rose campion (*Lychnis coronaria*), and assorted allium provide early July color in Elizabeth Luce's entry garden.

In Aquinnah Seth and Megan Woods have also created a charming garden near the entry to their home, but they've filled it with vegetables instead of perennials and shrubs. Because their property is extremely sandy, they have forgone a traditional lawn and planted American beach grass instead of turf.

Tucked in a sunny spot between the beach grass and the parking area is a tidy fenced garden planted in large boxes. These containers are separated by stacks of tinted cement tiles. Seth says that they found the tiles under their house, and he and Megan have piled them between the planting boxes to add the structure and color that give the tiny garden a sense of permanence.

The Woodses' vegetable garden is a good example of how a small garden can benefit from a formal, balanced layout. Although large spaces are a natural setting for informal or slightly wild gardens, smaller spaces are better suited for more circumscribed and composed plantings.

A wooden toolbox becomes a mini–garden shed near Seth and Megan Woods's vegetable garden, which overlooks the ocean in Aquinnah.

▲▲ This small garden is the epitome of summer in Malcolm and Jean Campbell's property in Vineyard Haven. Tucked behind the house, the zinnias, tomatoes, and herbs that surround the clothesline make this garden every bit as evocative of the season as the waterfront view from the front yard.

▲ Chard is one of the most ornamental and long-lasting crops one can grow in a vegetable garden, no matter what the size. This container garden, planted by Seth and Megan Woods, shows just how beautiful this leaf crop can be.

Rick and Roberta Gross love the soft, low-maintenance plantings that Steve Yaffee of Crosswater Landscapes installed around their Aquinnah home. Ornamental grasses such as these *Pennisetum* and *Miscanthus* combine beautifully with *Nepeta* 'Six Hills Giant' and *Sedum* 'Autumn Joy'.

The Soil . . . or Lack Thereof

People desire gardens for many reasons, but on the Vineyard it *isn't* the soil that encourages them to start planting. The land on Martha's Vineyard is the result of glacial moraines and an outwash plain that created large areas of sand, rocks, and clay for future gardeners to cope with. Some islanders garden in dense, heavy clay while others plant in a sandbox, and generations of farmers have hauled rocks of all sizes out of their fields.

Several gardeners in Vineyard Haven and Edgartown report that the soil on their properties has been planted and improved for so many years that they now have a good base in which to garden. Elsewhere on the island, however, people aren't as lucky.

"My biggest challenge is the soil," one gardener, Joan Svetz, confirms. "You've got to work at it!" Joan and her husband, John, garden in Oak Bluffs, and they amend their sandy soil with organic matter every year. Given this treatment, the sandy slope that was left after their house construction has been transformed into a terraced garden where roses, perennials, and small shrubs flourish.

When Paul Jackson digs a hole about eighteen inches deep, he quickly reveals how effective his constant soil amendments have been. The native ground is pure sand, but the upper layer of soil has become dark from Paul's continual applications of composted manure and plant material.

Although Dawn Greeley's property in Chilmark is also on an incline and sits where the glacier paused, she has clay on one side and rocks on the other. In fact, all the rocks in her hillside garden come from the property, and they provide the perfect setting to plant dwarf conifers and perennials.

Both clay and sand are improved by the addition of organic matter, and island gardeners use manure, seaweed, homemade or store-bought compost, leaves, grass clippings, and other organics to improve their soils. These amendments can be dug into the soil in new gardens or annual and vegetable beds. In established gardens they can be placed around the plants on the surface of the soil, so that over time they amend from the top down. Even the bark mulch that is frequently used to control weeds is beneficial for the soil.

Looking like watercolors sprung to life, the bearded iris in Joan Svetz's garden are made all the more enchanting by their short period of bloom.

Joan Svetz's garden is graced by the variegated willow (*Salix integra* 'Hakuro Nishiki'). This plant, which can be grown as a shrub or a tree, almost looks like it's covered with white flowers, but it is the white new foliage that is so striking. In June the willow is a lovely companion to blue perennial salvia (*Salvia nemorosa*) and sweet William (*Dianthus barbatus*).

Some gardeners find that layers of composted manure and seaweed, with a couple of inches of loam in between, will build up a bed of improved soil that can be planted fairly quickly. This method doesn't require any digging, and it works particularly well when several layers of amendments and loam are piled on top of sandy soil. A similar approach is often used to fill raised beds; the layers of topsoil and organic amendments do not necessarily need to be mixed together because they will be combined over time by planting, earthworms, and root growth.

Other island gardeners choose to till their amendments into the soil that nature has given them. Paul Jackson, for example, has been turning his amendments into his gardens for at least fifty years. Most of the nearly two acres that Paul and his wife, Mary, live on is gardened, so it's easy to imagine the large amounts of amendments that Paul has worked into the beds over the years.

A partially sunken greenhouse and several cold frames nurture and shelter the young plants before Paul Jackson puts them in his gardens. Next to the red wheelbarrow, the stalks of rhubarb plants grow, ready to be picked.

Paul Jackson mulches his trees with mounds of scallop shells. As they start to crumble, he moves them onto the driveway and replaces those around the trees with a fresh layer.

Mary Jackson raises cut flowers that are sold at local stores and at her stand on Edgartown–Vineyard Haven Road. On some days it's all she can do to keep the display cans at both locations filled with bouquets! But flowers aren't the only crop that grows in the Jacksons' soil: much of their food comes from their large vegetable garden, berry patches, and fruit trees.

The variety and amount of produce that Paul Jackson grows are so great that other gardeners on the island describe him as "incredible" and "an amazing gardener." His daughter Beverly Bergeron, who also grows and sells cut flowers, says that she learned about plants from growing up surrounded by their garden. "There isn't a fruit or nut that my parents didn't grow," she reports.

Paul credits much of his success as a gardener to the attention that he pays to the soil. He has routinely dumped horse manure, eelgrass, garden clippings, and leaves on the garden and tilled it under. "Also, we used to bury fish," he recalls. In addition to the soil amendments that are turned under in spring or fall, Paul sows winter rye over the gardens at the end of each growing season. Winter rye will germinate and grow even in cool fall temperatures, and this crop prevents his well-tilled and amended soil from blowing away over the winter. In the spring the rye gets tilled into the garden, supplying more organic matter and further enriching his soil.

Paul Jackson is wise to take the power of the wind seriously. The sea breeze that keeps the island cool in the summer is easily capable of carrying the earth away with every gust, especially in the winter, when the land has few plants to hold the soil in place.

Heavy rains can also wash soil away, especially when a garden is planted on an incline. After Dawn Greeley's house was built in Chilmark, she knew that the steep slope in front of the house would need planting around the rocks to control erosion. Dawn is an artist, and she says that although she'd never considered herself a gardener, she came to realize that planting the slope was composing with texture and color on a three-dimensional, living canvas. The rocks that provide the solidity and structure for the garden were already there.

In order to have large onions early in the season, Paul starts them in his greenhouse. When the seedlings are young and about six inches tall, he shears a couple of inches off the new foliage. This method works almost *too* well, Jackson says. "I got disqualified at the fair one year because my onions were too big!"

Peonies, salvia, and *Verbascum* bloom along the edge of the Jacksons' Edgartown driveway.

When it came to choosing plants that would complement the landscape, Dawn says, "I had good advice from experts and I *listened.*" Dawn sought help from Polly Hill and Carol Knapp, and one of the recommendations that they gave her was about spacing dwarf conifers well apart. "I put in annuals, perennials, and grasses to fill in between the conifers; then as the shrubs grew I'd remove the grasses or perennials, or stop planting the annuals," Dawn explains.

Planting the small conifers a good distance from each other was smart because even the slowest-growing plants do grow larger. Now the assorted colors and textures of the evergreens, contrasting with the sturdiness of the native boulders, create a beautiful, low-maintenance garden on the hillside in front of the house.

Garden Choreography

Susanne Clark's garden was also planted on a slope, but on this property the native stone was used to build walls and create a terraced garden. Susanne and her husband, Ben, selected their Chilmark lot because they loved the agricultural setting, the decent soil, and the south-facing hillside where Susanne planned to place her garden.

Ben Clark's profession is architectural restoration and preservation, and their home, part of which was built in

◄◄ Native stone, dwarf conifers, and perennials fill the low-maintenance slope in Dawn Greeley's garden. Dawn listened to advice about spacing the shrubs well apart and filling in with perennials and annuals. Now that the shrubs have grown, there is little need for fill-in plants.

◄ One of Susanne Clark's challenges is the high amount of minerals in her water. She says that the water not only turns her stones a rusty color, but leaves fuzzy foliage like lamb's ears looking dirty. Fortunately, other plants are unaffected.

▼ Susanne Clark designed her garden using inspiration from a Gertrude Jekyll design. Jekyll (1843–1932) was an author, garden designer, photographer, and plantswoman who is remembered for her painterly approach to garden design. Clark emulated Jekyll's arrangement of hot-colored flowers transitioning to a bed with the blues, lavenders, and pinks seen here.

1730, was originally located off New Lane in West Tisbury. Ben and his nephew Bradford disassembled it, documenting and numbering all the boards so that it could be reassembled in a new location.

Inspiration for the layout and style of the garden came from a plan made by the English designer Gertrude Jekyll in the 1920s. Susanne, who studied landscape design at the Radcliffe program and has designed historically accurate gardens for others, created her garden using some features from the Jekyll garden and some of her own.

Because plants are constantly growing, and because perennials come in and out of bloom through the season, Susanne thinks of the garden-planning process as choreography rather than design. Like dancers in a ballet, each plant plays a role, sometimes combining with others in complex arrangements of foliage and flowers, and sometimes taking a starring role on the garden stage.

In order to choreograph this succession of growth and change, Susanne used an unusual method to plan her garden. She laid out a drawing of the beds on two boards, using a scale of one inch to one foot. Then she cut out circular pictures of the various plants that she planned on using, making the size of the circles correspond to the general mature size of the plant. On the back of these disks she placed various colors such as gray, lime, or dark green, to represent the foliage of the plant that was pictured on the front of the circle. On this side she also wrote the time when the plant would be in bloom.

Crocosmia, Asiatic lilies, daylilies, and *Gaillardia* are just a few of the perennials in Susanne Clark's "hot border."

Using the board and these disks, Susanne could arrange the plants and turn foliage- or flower-side up to see the changes of flowers and leaves though the season. "This is an absolutely fanatical way to do it," Susanne admits, but it let her plan a garden that was colorful and interesting before anything was actually planted. And just as we often get as much enjoyment from the planning of a vacation as we do from the trip itself, Susanne's method allowed her to savor her garden long before the plants went into the ground or came into bloom.

Once her garden was planted, Susanne came up with a

Charles and Martha Schmidt continue to enjoy the *Narcissus* planted over a hundred years ago by a former owner, Professor Nathaniel Southgate Shaler, from Boston. When the professor took walks around the property, he carried a stash of bulbs in his pocket. Periodically he'd stop and stick a few in the ground, and today these clumps of daffodils thrive in the woods and on the hillsides overlooking the sea.

way to rate the 115 perennials she is growing. Once a week she goes into the garden and gives each plant a score. "For foliage only, plants earn a score from zero to three," she explains, "with the majority getting a zero. For bloom, the scores range from one to five, with five the highest available score even for an exceptional foliage plant in full bloom. These scores are entered into a spreadsheet."

Although it might seem like a great deal of work, this routine provides a way to evaluate every plant's performance with a clear eye. "I created this scoring system initially so I could tell, by the fireside in the dead of winter, when and for how long each plant put on a show," Susanne says. "This enables me to decide what plants remain in the garden." She goes on to say that the spreadsheet is useful when adjustments are needed as well. Susanne can see which perennials are in bloom at any given time, so if one needs transplanting

Susanne Clark's Top Twelve Perennials for Sun

The following perennials received the highest rating in Susanne Clark's weekly scoring system. Susanne points out that because she judges her plants on the basis of both flowering and foliage, seven of the top twelve are there because of leaf color or texture, and the effectiveness of these plants largely depends on their placement. Putting plants with colorful foliage adjacent to green-leaved selections ensures visual interest whether the plants are in bloom or not.

Geranium 'Rozanne'. Because this perennial geranium blooms profusely from mid-June to mid-October, it tops Susanne's list. 'Rozanne' is a recently introduced cultivar that has round, violet-blue flowers on slightly sprawling stems. The deep-green leaves are lightly marbled with chartreuse and grow in mounds that are attractive before the flowers appear. 'Rozanne' is a low spreader, attaining a width of five feet by mid-August. Although Susanne reports that she usually has continuous flower production, these plants can be cut back to the ground if flowering falters in hot weather or if the foliage starts to look straggly.

Gaillardia 'Fanfare' (Fanfare blanket flower). Another prolific bloomer, 'Fanfare' also begins flowering in mid-June and sustains strong bloom into October. Susanne has planted this perennial at the front of the border, where she says that it makes a neat, mounded presentation. "I use its red and yellow trumpetlike petals to tie together the reds and yellows of the hot section of the borders," Susanne explains. Regular deadheading is needed to promote continual flowering, but Susanne says that it's not too time-consuming.

Ajuga reptans 'Burgundy Glow' (carpet bugleweed). This plant, usually used as a groundcover, earns its high score with its colorful leaves, which are effective from early May through October. Foliage is everything with this plant: although it blooms in May, the flowers are insignificant. The leaves, however, are a colorful mix of gray-green, magenta-purple, and cream, and they form a tapestry of color that complements other plants throughout the season. Like all ajuga varieties, 'Burgundy Glow' will spread, but Susanne says that it's easy to edit out any unwanted plants.

Tanacetum parthenium 'Aureum' (golden feverfew). Susanne appreciates this short-lived perennial because the fernlike, chartreuse-yellow leaves make a statement from April into October. Growing lower than the common feverfew, the golden variety tops out between 8 and 12 inches tall and is crowned with white and yellow, button-like flowers beginning in July. Golden feverfew self-sows around the garden, so it should be edited and transplanted annually.

Liriope muscari 'Silver Sunproof' (variegated lily-turf). Starting in mid-May, the grasslike leaves of this variegated *Liriope* provide a color and texture in contrast to neighboring plants. "I use the low clumps of 'Silver Sunproof' as an edging," Susanne says. "From a distance the leaves, which are striped lengthwise with green and yellow to cream, appear cream-colored." Blue flower spikes resembling long grape hyacinths appear in late summer. Because this plant has attractive foliage all summer and does not require deadheading, it is a low-maintenance perennial.

Gaura lindhelmeri 'Whirling Butterflies' and 'So White' (butterfly gaura). This plant is a North American native that is both long-blooming and easy to grow. It begins to flower in June and continues into October. If flower production begins to fade at the end of July, cutting the flower stalks off to just above the foliage will spur the plant to bloom well into the fall. 'Whirling Butterflies' has white flowers tinged with pale pink and will grow to 3 1/2 feet tall and wide. 'So White', as the name suggests, is pure white. "The delicate haze of *Gaura* in bloom provides a foil for more substantive blooms nearby," Clark says. Like many perennials that flower for a long period, *Gaura* may be short-lived, and it needs excellent drainage through the winter months in order to survive.

Stachys byzantina (lamb's ears). The traditional lamb's ears makes a dense clump of soft, hairy, silver-gray leaves that are effective for the entire season. Silvery, wooly stems grow upright in June, and the bees love the tiny magenta-pink flowers that appear in July. Although the flowers are small, they are a traditional component of English cottage gardens or moon gardens. Along the edge of a border,

or if she's adding new varieties to the garden, she can take full advantage of knowing where to find complementary flower colors, contrasting foliage, and shapes that will flatter the transplants and new additions.

An Abundance of Stone

There are stone walls everywhere on Martha's Vineyard, and they are one of the highlights that give island gardens a sense of place. Whether they are held together with cement or dry-stacked (constructed without mortar), native stone walls often line Vineyard fields, encircle patios, and enclose vegetable or flower gardens. What has been a continual frustration to farmers throughout the centuries has provided this island with one of its more charming features.

Vineyard Variety

Although the use of native stone is common throughout the island, one of the things that makes Martha's Vineyard

Stachys byzantina is a wonderful contrast to the green plants nearby.

Sedum 'Frosty Morn' (variegated stonecrop). The cream-edged apple-green leaves of this sedum add contrast and color to Susanne's border from early May to October. Like other sedums, this one is drought-tolerant and grows best when not given an abundance of fertilizer. In late August and September pink and cream flowers add subtle late-season color. 'Frosty Morn' grows up to 2 feet tall by 2 feet wide. New growth on this variegated plant can easily revert to all green, and gardeners should remove any non-variegated growth as soon as it appears.

Aster lateriflorus 'Lady in Black' (black-leaved calico aster). "The black-purple bushy mound of foliage of 'Lady in Black' shows to good effect beginning in May," Susanne says, "if the rabbits don't eat it." In addition to the dark foliage in early summer, in autumn the plant's covered with a cloud of tiny, daisylike white flowers with raspberry centers. Susanne reports that although this plant reaches a height of 4 feet in

her garden, she doesn't find staking necessary. Many asters can be prone to powdery mildew and browning leaves on the lower stems, but this variety is more resistant to both of these problems. Other than periodic division, it requires no maintenance and is quite drought-tolerant as well.

Nepeta X faassenii (catmint). "This *Nepeta* begins to bloom in early May," Susanne notes, "reaches peak performance in the second half of May, and then continues to contribute with varying intensity through October." The catmints are long-blooming, drought-tolerant perennials with small, gray-green leaves. This variety is low growing and has lavender-blue flowers on short spikes. After the initial burst of bloom, the plant benefits from cutting out the older foliage or shearing it down. Like most gray-foliaged plants, it is not usually attractive to rabbits and deer.

Iris ensata 'Variegata' (variegated Japanese iris). Although this iris contributes reddish-purple blooms for a couple of weeks in late June to early July, Susanne says that it earns its place in this list because of its attractive grasslike foliage. The leaves are vertically striped with bands of cream and blue-green, and the plant remains attractive the entire season. This foliage accent plant can be grown at waterside or in pots sitting in water. "While it needs ample moisture until it blooms," Susanne notes, "mine does just fine in the border where it receives the same amount of water as the other plants." All iris benefit from spring or fall division every four years.

Salvia verticillata 'Purple Rain' (whorled sage). 'Purple Rain' salvia is at peak bloom in mid-June through July, but Susanne says that hers continues to bloom, although with decreasing effect, into October when deadheaded regularly. This perennial plant forms a bushy mound of fuzzy, olive-green leaves and has spikes of violet-purple flowers. Growing to 18 inches tall, it requires full sun and well-drained soil. Like other salvias, 'Purple Rain' can be cut to the ground whenever it reaches a point when it is no longer an asset in the garden.

Because the Vineyard's temperatures are moderated by the surrounding ocean, Martha Schmidt can grow early-spring-blooming camellias.

▼ Instead of an umbrella, Lew French has placed a twig sculpture in the stone table, and the chairs sit on a carpet of thyme in a garden designed by Carly Look.

The talents of Lew French, a stone artist, and the garden designer Carly Look come together in this Chilmark garden. This outdoor shower is next to a pool, with an arbor and hillside gardens to the sides.

so interesting is that each town has an individual personality. Homes in Edgartown are normally white clapboard whaling captains' houses with black shutters, built in the 1800s. Oak Bluffs is filled with colorfully painted gingerbread cottages and Victorian-style architecture, whereas up-island dwellings are frequently covered with gray cedar shingles. West Tisbury and Chilmark retain a very rural character, and the lower-growing vegetation and often smaller houses of Aquinnah speak to the exposure to off-ocean winds.

As might be expected, the styles of gardens in these towns vary as well. Edgartown gardens tend to be more formal in their layout. Sheared privet hedges and boxwood borders are seen throughout town; roses and hydrangeas reign in late June and early July, and dahlias and other annuals provide color through September.

In Oak Bluffs the color is amped-up, as flowers compete with the lively paint colors used on the Victorian houses

and cottages. Here it is uncertain which is more vibrant, the buildings or the landscaping. And in general, gardens seem to become less formal as you move from Vineyard Haven through pastoral West Tisbury, Chilmark, and farther up-island.

▲ The familiar 'Annabelle' hydrangea (*Hydrangea arborescens* 'Annabelle') grows next to the less well-known *Hydrangea serrata* 'Miyama-yae-murasaki' in a Chilmark plant collector's garden.

◀ Annuals, perennials, shrubs, and roses fill the informally planted beds around Bob and Judy Jahries' home and greenhouse in West Tisbury.

This summer-fresh hardy hibiscus (*Hibiscus moscheutos* 'Blue River II') grows about six feet tall in Peggy and Stephen Zablotny's garden in Vineyard Haven.

▲ The midsummer bounty in the Jahrieses' vegetable garden includes zinnias, dahlias, and raspberries as well as vegetables.

▼ Chard and a trellis of peas grow where there's a view of stone fences and the Chilmark coastline beyond.

Homegrown

Often included in island landscapes is a vegetable garden, and Vineyard gardeners are accomplished in creating gardens that are beautiful and productive. One look at all the fruit and vegetable entries at the agricultural fair every August shows how popular home food production is on the island. And just as there are many ways to create a flower-bed, there are countless ways to fit fruits and vegetables into the landscape.

One island gardener has tucked her garden on a south-facing Chilmark hillside. Locating a garden in the middle of a slope, especially if it faces south or southwest, can provide a sheltered spot for heat-loving vegetables such as tomatoes, eggplant, and peppers. Such a site will have soil that is faster to warm in the spring and, because cold air sinks, some protection from the first early frosts of autumn. The chilly air that will kill tender plants on cold fall nights will flow down the slope, collecting in the low land and leaving garden produce untouched for a few more days.

Because sufficient sunlight is essential for growing vegetables, most gardeners locate their veggie beds wherever the sun is strongest. This might be in any portion of the yard, in raised beds and boxes, or in containers on the deck. In Paul Jackson's case, his garden fills most of the property, in front of the house, in the backyard, and along both sides. This suits the Jacksons very well, but those who are not as willing or able to grow most of their food site their gardens to take advantage of the sun or in a sheltered location.

▲ Celeste Stickney makes good use of deck space by planting railing boxes with salad greens and upside-down plant hangers with cherry tomatoes.

◄ The round shape of this vegetable garden seemed to fit naturally into the Chilmark hillside, and the gardener built the fence out of recycled materials.

▼ Dahlias provide late-summer color in Arnold Zack's vegetable garden in Aquinnah.

Finding What Works

Gardeners on the Vineyard are frequently pushing the limits. Perhaps the inspiration to see which marginally hardy plants will survive comes from Polly Hill, or maybe gardeners are just intrigued about expanding their palette of plants. Whatever the reason, the penchant for growing things that normally don't survive this far north thrives on the island.

Because Martha's Vineyard is totally surrounded by water, the winter temperatures are even more moderate than they are on much of Cape Cod and coastal New England. This allows gardeners to use a wider range of plants and to experiment with growing varieties that usually don't live so far north.

Those willing to test plants do so in a variety of ways. Some place tender species in protected areas, some grow many plants from seed, and some use winter protection as plants get established. Every property has microclimates, and most have warmer, sheltered spots—an area next to the house that warms earlier in the spring, for example. Plants grown in such places may be shielded enough to make it through all but the coldest winters.

◄ The poet's daffodil is an old favorite that is ideal for naturalizing. *Narcissus poeticus* blooms later than many daffodils, and the flowers are extremely fragrant. Martha Schmidt is fortunate to have hundreds that bloom in her yard.

► This hillside of poet's narcissus (*Narcissus poeticus*), with its display of flowers that carpet the slope next to the Schmidts' home, calls to mind the famous Wordsworth verse.

►► *Phlox paniculata*, *Echinacea*, and *Verbena bonariensis* predominate in the charming border outside Abigail Higgins's vegetable garden.

▼ A millstone is surrounded by assorted thymes and other creeping plants in a beautiful Katama garden designed and planted by Peggy Schwier. In addition to the lovely mix of colors and textures in and around this patio, Peggy has skillfully blended the property into the wild surroundings by planting large groups of ornamental grasses and native plants.

▲ Rose of Sharon makes a colorful hedge in front of Hope Wipple's porch in Edgartown.

▶ In the profusion of perennials in the Wipple garden, Jeff Verner, a professional gardener, usually includes something little-known or unique, and Hope enjoys trying to discover the mystery plants' identities.

▲ This perennial border developed over the course of fifteen years, says Joyce Maxner, who explains that her husband, Steve, shaped and dug the bed a bit at a time. The colorful buoys on the shed and edging of rocks add a delightful sense of place to the assortment of perennials.

◄ From mid-June through September Jeff Verner keeps Hope Wipple's garden filled with flowers. Here the repetition of 'Moonbeam' coreopsis unifies the border with long-lasting, butter-yellow blooms.

▼ Although this beautiful perennial border looks finished to the casual eye, the gardener, Joyce Maxner, knows that even a full cottage-style garden needs constant tending. Editing, dividing, and deadheading are just some of the tasks that Joyce does in this front-yard garden. She says that she sees the garden as a work in progress, and although it takes time and effort, it's the best kind of work there is.

Growing plants from seed allows for the possibility that some of the seedlings might be hardier than others, so this is one method of selecting a plant that is more resilient than another of the same species. Providing some protection in the form of mulch, pine boughs, or floating row cover can help young plants grow stronger so they can be evaluated for winter hardiness.

▶ The Suhlers' visitors are welcomed with a cheerful wagon of flowering plants.

▼ By combining annuals and perennials, Rick Hoffman makes sure that this patio garden is filled with color through the entire summer.

▲ Rick Hoffman, an artist and professional gardener, designed and maintains this perennial garden for a client in Chilmark.

▶ Charlotte and John Suhler's garden faces the water, so the plants are exposed to the wind. Donna Kelly, a professional gardener from Edgartown who designs and maintains the Suhlers' gardens, has filled this bed with sturdy annuals and perennials that will flower despite the exposed location.

Sara Jane Sylvia has created the perfect summer setting with a tumble of flowering perennials and a gazebo complete with chandelier. The artist-gardener Rick Hoffman assists Sara with the gardens.

Chapter 2

ISLAND RICHES

Aside from the individual gardens, Martha's Vineyard is filled with sources of materials, inspiration, and information. The island contains several nurseries and garden centers, lovely beds and plantings around island businesses, and two public gardens that are esteemed in the horticultural world and cherished by all who visit.

Island garden centers carry a huge selection of plants, ranging from the tried and true to the new and unique. Some nurseries grow a portion of their own stock, a few specialize in particular types of plants, and many offer a complete assortment of annuals, perennials, shrubs, and trees throughout the growing season.

Flower-filled gardens surround many island businesses, from hotels and bed-and-breakfasts to farm stands and shops. Colorful annuals fill small beds in front of many stores in Vineyard Haven and line the walkways to restaurants in Edgartown. Throughout the summer and early fall, Martha's Vineyard is in bloom.

The Martha's Vineyard Garden Club is a valuable source of horticultural inspiration and information for island gardeners. The garden club offers educational meetings, as well as hands-on experience through opportunities to volunteer for garden-related projects. Members install and maintain gardens in public places and propagate plants in their greenhouse at the Wakeman Center, off Lamberts Cove Road.

From October to May the club members gather at the greenhouse on Monday mornings to tend to the plants.

The beautiful placement of the plants at Mytoi, and the assorted colors and textures of foliage, attracts people who come to stroll, meditate, or paint.

▲▲ A sign at Donaroma's Nursery in Edgartown invites visitors to investigate the greenhouse.

▲ The storefront at Eden is always bursting with color. This Vineyard Haven garden center is kept well stocked with plants from April through the growing season.

▲ The Kwanzan cherry (*Prunus serrulata* 'Kwanzan') next to Donaroma's Nursery raises everyone's spirits when it's covered with bubblegum-pink flowers in May.

◄▲ Echinacea and hundreds of other flowering and nonflowering plants put on a show in every section of Heather Gardens in West Tisbury.

▲ Jardin Mahoney is a full-service garden center on Edgartown–Vineyard Haven Road in Oak Bluffs. The display tables are always filled with colorful seasonal flowers.

◄ According to its Web site, Vineyard Gardens started in 1980, when Chuck Wiley began helping Nina Schneider with her lawn and gardens. Now a full-service garden center, Vineyard Gardens is filled with beautiful plants and displays.

▲ The landscape gardener Jeff Verner plants a kaleidoscope of color that borders the walkway to L'étoile restaurant in Edgartown.

◄ Many hotels and bed-and-breakfasts on the island have beautiful gardens. This one at the Harborside Inn, in Edgartown, is planted and maintained by Sarah Stock.

◄▲ For seven years Joanne Leighton has displayed and sold garden antiques at Abby-Ems in Edgartown.

▲ The shutters and trim at Larsen's fish market in Menemsha are as colorful as the flowers that fill the boxes.

◄ The Japanese pagoda tree (*Sophora japonica*) is notable because it blooms in late summer and is filled with interesting, pale green seedpods in the fall. This large specimen in front of the Edgartown Public Library is impressive from a distance and in silhouette against the summer sky.

Seeds are sown and cuttings are taken, which are sold at their spring plant sale. The club has also propagated plants for Polly Hill Arboretum sales. Summer residents are not excluded from the benefits of this organization because, unlike most garden clubs, this organization continues to meet throughout the year.

Garden club members and others take full advantage of the two island gardens that are open to the public. Both Mytoi and Polly Hill Arboretum are important resources for all Vineyard residents and must-see attractions for visitors.

Mytoi

Let me make a suggestion: when you visit Mytoi for the first time, walk around the entire garden *twice*. Yes, you should take the guide map when you arrive, and follow the plan as you stroll around the garden. Should you want to learn which plants people commonly inquire about, follow the diagram past all the numbered trees. Then return the map and walk through the garden again. *Slowly.* You will have a completely different encounter the second time around. It is worth making that subsequent trip, for then you'll experience the true scope and purpose of this garden.

◀ Plants that have been propagated by members of the Martha's Vineyard Garden Club wait for the end of winter in the Wakeman Center greenhouse.

▲ The Vineyard's spring air may be chilly, but every Monday members of the Martha's Vineyard Garden Club spend a morning in this warm, flower-filled paradise.

▶ Many plants can be propagated by taking stem or leaf cuttings. These are being started by members of the Martha's Vineyard Garden Club.

Mytoi is not about learning which new shrubs and trees you can plant in your landscape, although you certainly can do that there. It's not about beds of dazzlingly bright annual flowers or English perennial borders. And finally, it's not a replica of a traditional Japanese garden, although it has elements of, and inspiration from, such plantings. To my mind, Mytoi is all about seeing, slowing down, and being in the moment.

Today's garden is completely different from the original that was planted in the late 1950s. Most gardens and gardeners have to accept change, and Mytoi is no exception. Mary Wakeman originally bought land on Chappaquiddick where she was to build a summerhouse, and it came with a three-acre property across the street. She hired Hugh Jones, who was an architect in Edgartown, to create the plans, and

she later sold the three-acre plot to him for one dollar. Jones created a Japanese-style garden on the land, and when he died in 1965 his heirs sold it back to the Wakeman family, with the agreement that it would be kept open to the public.

Mary Wakeman gave this original garden, along with an endowment that would pay for its upkeep, to the Trustees of Reservations in 1976. Eleven more acres of land was donated in 1981, and the Japanese-inspired garden remained open to the public. In 1991, however, Hurricane Bob devastated this pine-shaded landscape.

During the hurricane, several properties on Chappaquiddick experienced microburst winds, which are small, very intense downdrafts that are capable of causing significant damage. Many trees at Mytoi were uprooted, and

▲ Although most weeds are pulled at Mytoi, occasionally a wild plant or two are allowed to stay. This mullein (*Verbascum thapsus*) stands like a sentinel above the pond.

◀ After Hurricane Bob destroyed the original garden, the community came together to clear out the damage before new shrubs, trees, and perennials were planted at Mytoi.

what was once a shady garden became a debris-filled mess. Once the wreckage was cleared, only a few shrubs and trees remained, and the land was open to the sun.

Mytoi was redesigned and restored through the talents and dedication of three people: Don Sibley, Julie Moir Messervy, and Lindsay Allison. The Trustees hired Don because of his knowledge of Japanese gardens. Don is an artist who has lived in Japan and has a wide range of experiences with both plants and design. Lindsay Allison had been a volunteer gardener at Mytoi since 1986, and as a summer resident at Chappaquiddick she had been visiting the gar-

den since she was a girl. The Trustees also hired Julie Moir Messervy, a well-known landscape designer and author, to provide a master plan for the renovation of the storm-torn garden.

Julie was the perfect person to develop a plan for this garden because of her interest in how landscapes can provide personal journeys of reflection and renewal. Gardens that are open to the public have particular challenges that private gardens don't, and Julie is especially talented in designing a garden so that it elicits the desired behavior from the public.

The birch-lined shady entry to Mytoi prompts people to quiet down and enjoy a peaceful walk through the gardens.

Don, Lindsay, and Julie wanted people to slow down and truly experience Mytoi. Garden designers struggle with how they can prompt people to pay attention to the spirit of the landscape without chiding them with an array of warnings and signs. At Mytoi this was masterfully accomplished in several ways.

The land was divided into a series of garden rooms, so that visitors are presented with small, intimate spaces and broader vistas. Paths are frequently narrow, forcing people to slow down and walk in single file. The bridge, which Don designed to replace the original garden's signature red arched structure, does not go straight across the pond, which is the centerpiece of the garden. And there are several places to sit and enjoy the views.

Even the entry to Mytoi was designed by Julie Messervy to help people make the transition from the bustle of traveling to Chappaquiddick to the serenity of the garden. After passing through a Japanese-style gate that was built of local black locust, you walk through a grove of trees that includes carefully spaced birches. "The birch walk has several purposes," Don Sibley explains. "People tend to quiet down in a shady woods." The simplicity and tranquillity of the entry also help to set the tone of reflection that contributes to a full enjoyment of the garden.

People who are used to visiting arboreta and botanical gardens where all plants are labeled may be puzzled about the lack of such name tags at Mytoi. This was a careful and wise decision made by the designers and the board, because when people are presented with text they tend to read the signs instead of experiencing the garden. It is the color and

▲ At Mytoi, dividing some areas into small garden rooms and creating other expansive vistas has encouraged people to slow down and *really look* at the composition of plants.

▶ Plants, pond, and sky guarantee that a visit to Mytoi will be pleasant no matter what the weather.

texture of each plant, and the *juxtaposition* of those plants, that we are meant to notice. It is the experience of moving through this lovely island oasis, what it prompts us to remember, and how it makes us *feel* that are special here.

Since the reconstruction, Don Sibley has remained as head gardener and has designed and built the garden's structures. These include the locust gates and a small shel-

ter that is modeled after a Japanese *azumaya*, which is an arbor or covered area often found in traditional teahouses and gardens.

Lindsay Allison continues to contribute her time and design skills to Mytoi as well. She is particularly involved with the planting of annuals and perennials in the garden. Lindsay and Don have been the principal designers and

This bridge was designed by Don Sibley to replace the signature red bridge that originally spanned the pond at Mytoi. The bridge was purposefully designed not to go straight across, so that people are encouraged to slow down and observe the pond and garden instead of hurrying directly from one side to the other.

gardeners for the past sixteen years, although they have assistance from paid laborers and willing volunteers.

In fact, the way that the residents of Chappaquiddick and the Vineyard have come together to support Mytoi is a magical aspect of this garden that visitors do not see. From the post-hurricane clearing to the yearly spring cleanups and annual restocking of the pond's resident koi, community volunteers demonstrate their appreciation of this island treasure. The people of Chappaquiddick are also consistently generous about financially supporting special projects and funding other expenses.

But that's not to say that the garden is without trials. Like other nonprofit institutions, the Trustees of Reservations are challenged by rising costs and tight budgets. They depend heavily on people such as Don and Lindsay, who devote their time and talents to the garden out of love and with little remuneration. Once these two move on to other

pursuits, it will be difficult to find replacements willing to be so hands-on in a largely volunteer position.

One daily management issue is not having enough help to get to all of the garden maintenance. "You have to keep up a certain level of attention," Don Sibley states, "and that's the biggest long-term problem." For, although visitors see the beautifully arranged plants, what they don't see is the amount of effort that it takes to keep the garden attractive. Shrubs and trees must be pruned, debris cleared away, and weeds pulled.

In addition to regular editing of weeds and self-sown plants, shrubs and trees must occasionally be removed as well. Don explains that deleting certain plants is important for maintaining good composition in a garden. "For example," he says, "if a plant has gotten too big for its location, so that it blurs what is happening in that area instead of adding to it, that plant may need to go. I've learned that it's

▲ Camellias (*Camellia japonica*) are well-known evergreen shrubs in warmer climates, but it is obvious that they thrive on the Vineyard as well. This camellia flowers in the spring at Polly Hill Arboretum.

◄ Polly Hill Arboretum is located on State Road in West Tisbury. The sign marking the entrance also gives information about hours and special events.

okay to say, 'We've appreciated you for a number of years, but now it's time . . . ,' and I've gotten much better about using the chainsaw when it's needed."

Learning to embrace change is but one lesson that this unique garden has to share. Some come to Mytoi to meditate or paint. Others travel here to experience the blending of a Japanese and Chappaquiddick sensibility, or to appreciate plants and nature. All this and more can be experienced at Mytoi, and those who make their way here will be delighted by this lovely garden.

Polly Hill Arboretum

Polly Hill is a beautiful but unassuming arboretum where more is going on than immediately meets the eye. This garden in West Tisbury is a tremendous resource for island residents and the horticultural world far beyond the Vineyard, but the chance visitor might overlook

its unique history and the importance of what currently takes place.

Purchased as a summer home for Polly's parents, Margaret and Howard Butcher Jr., the original forty acres of land was christened "Barnard's Inn Farm," after one of the previous owners. Polly and her husband, Julian, inherited the farm, and at the age of fifty Polly became intrigued with growing trees and the possibility of turning the property into an arboretum.

In 1958 Polly Hill began planting seeds in a nursery bed on the farm. One of her first goals was to find a tree that could replace the island's Japanese black pines (*Pinus thunbergii*), which were dying. Native to coastal Japan, this tree had commonly been used for windbreaks on the Vineyard, but insects and diseases were killing the trees on the island and elsewhere in the United States. This quest for other windbreak plants led her to an interest in pines and

other trees, and soon Polly began to plant a wide range of genera and species.

Many of the plants that Polly grew were not known to be hardy as far north as the Vineyard, but she demonstrated that they would survive and even flourish on the island. In addition to pushing the limits of winter hardiness, Polly also selected seedlings that had characteristics that were unique among plants of the same species. These plants were frequently named for family members and grown not only on the twenty acres that Polly cultivated, but also at nurseries and other public gardens throughout the world.

Polly Hill's life is indeed an inspiring example of the power of an individual to make a difference in the world. In the pursuit of a personal passion, horticulture, she created a place of beauty, dozens of new shrubs and trees, and an organization that nurtures people as well as plants. It is inspirational to know that Polly Hill didn't start to grow and select plants until she was in her fifties, and that through her sixties and beyond she was still starting seeds and growing plants that would take many years to mature. This dedication and optimism are part of the history of this property that a casual tourist may not discover.

What everyone will encounter is a Vineyard property complete with lichen-covered stone walls and classic island architecture. There are open fields and shrub borders. There is an allée made of kousa dogwoods (*Cornus kousa*) and an arbor made of living hornbeam trees (*Carpinus*

▲ Polly's Play Pen was created so that Polly Hill could grow plants in an area where the deer and other creatures couldn't destroy her specimens.

◀ A beautiful fern-leaf European beech (*Fagus sylvatica* 'Asplenifolia') grows near a row of camellias and rhododendrons at Polly Hill.

▼ Plant lovers will always find a few "must-have" plants at the sale table at the entrance to Polly Hill Arboretum.

betulus var. *columnaris*). There is a beautiful, flower-filled garden called the Homestead Border between the house and the road, and there are countless mature specimens of shrubs and trees that most people never see in ordinary landscapes. And there is Polly's Play Pen, a fenced area that is 35 feet wide by 286 feet long. The Play Pen was made to keep out rabbits and deer, and it contains a combination of Polly's plant introductions and a wide assortment of rare and remarkable species.

At Polly Hill Arboretum (PHA) all the plants are labeled, which makes it easy to learn about shrubs and trees even when wandering solo on the grounds. There are also regular guided tours for those interested in learning about the arboretum's collections. Don't expect to see a bright

▲ When visiting Polly Hill Arboretum, be sure to enjoy the play of sun and shadow in the allée of kousa dogwood (*Cornus kousa*) trees. Several of these dogwoods are Polly's introductions.

◄ A northern catalpa (*Catalpa speciosa*) hangs over the stone wall at Polly Hill. Also blooming in midsummer is the bed of daylilies that lines the wall opposite the Far Barn, which is used for classes and special events.

Polly Hill's Plant Introductions

In her years working with plants in West Tisbury, Polly Hill selected or developed eighty-three plants with distinctive characteristics. Because of Polly, named varieties of *Abies, Chamaecyparis, Clematis, Cornus, Ilex, Juniperus, Magnolia, Malus, Oxydendrum, Rhododendron,* and *Stewartia* grace gardens throughout the world. Many of these plants were named for Polly's family members and friends, and she wrote a book about her introductions that will be published by the arboretum at a future date. Listed here are just a few of Polly Hill's plants.

Clematis 'Gabrielle'. This *Clematis* has lavender-blue flowers in May and June, and it often repeat-blooms in September. Growing 8 to 10 feet tall, this vine does well in full or part sun.

Cornus kousa 'Blue Shadow' (hybrid). The foliage of this kousa dogwood is very dark green with a tinge of blue. Proven to be heat-tolerant as well, 'Blue Shadow' also displays excellent yellow fall color. Other features include blossoming at an early age and occasional white bracts appearing with the pink or red fruit in late summer. 'Blue Shadow' grows to about 30 feet tall and 20 feet wide. Plant this kousa dogwood in full or part sun.

Ilex opaca 'Villanova'. Although *Ilex opaca* is native to Martha's Vineyard, this named variety originated off-island. Polly Hill recorded that Howard Butcher III spotted this selection of American holly growing in a lawn. He dug it out of the turf and moved it to his garden in Villanova, Pennsylvania. As a young plant it had leaves that were much wider than the norm, and as it grew it was shown to be a female that produced bright yellow berries. There are four 'Villanova' hollies currently growing near the Visitor Center at Polly Hill.

Malus 'Louisa' (hybrid). This small crabapple tree has a beautiful weeping form that grows around 15 feet high and wide. It has proven to have good to excellent disease resistance. In addition to its weeping habit, 'Louisa' provides several seasons of color, from its pink flowers in the spring to its bright yellow-orange fall color and yellow fruit.

Oxydendrum arboreum 'Chameleon'. This form of the native sourwood tree grows to 20 feet high and is valued for the pendulous clusters of white flowers that grace the plant in July. Like others of its species, this variety has beautiful fall foliage color in shades of red, yellow, and purple. 'Chameleon' is hardy to zone 5.

Rhododendron atlanticum 'Marydel'. Although this plant was originally thought to be a cross (*atlanticum* X *periclymenoides*), many now think that it is a particularly fine example of *R. atlanticum*. 'Marydel' is deciduous and has fragrant pink flowers in the spring. This shrub is winter-hardy to zone 5 and grows to be about 5 feet tall.

green monoculture lawn, however. Tim Boland, director at PHA, explains that this wouldn't be in keeping with the philosophy at the arboretum. "We have a Vineyard lawn, part grass, part wild weeds," Boland says. "We promote sustainable horticulture, so we use organic fertilizers and do not use lawn herbicides or irrigate turf. These practices are counterintuitive, lead to pollution of our one island aquifer, and are not in keeping with good land stewardship."

Preserving the island's resources, including water and plants, is one of the arboretum's missions and future goals. In the area of plant conservation and research, PHA wants to continue to document and monitor rare plant populations on the island and update and expand its flora. PHA is committed to working to restore old agricultural fields through the planting of native sand-plain grassland species, and to manage these fields with either controlled burning or seasonal mowing to restrain woody plant succession.

Other goals of PHA include continuing to bring in educators in horticulture, botany, and garden-interest topics for the Summer Lecture Series, and building a horticultural library and establishing a Master Gardener training program. Informing the public about invasive plants and the threat they pose to the local ecology and promoting the ideals of putting the right plant in the right place are also arboretum objectives.

New plants play a role in the future of PHA as well. Expanded plant collections that include specimens from Japan and native plants of the Atlantic coastal plain are on the list of goals, as is some future growth. "We intend to expand our collections with a new woodland garden area," Tim Boland says, "and to use our new greenhouse facility to grow and develop new plant varieties for garden introduction."

Such valuable and wide-ranging plans need funding, however, and this is probably the arboretum's biggest chal-

lenge. "Martha's Vineyard has many not-for-profits competing for available dollars," Tim Boland explains. "While Polly's story is inspiring to everyone who visits here, it is hard to garner support for an outdoor tree and shrub museum. People in general do not entirely comprehend the value of plants to our survival."

Funding aside, it's also hard for many to understand the challenges of just keeping things growing at Polly Hill. Thomas Clark, the Collections and Grounds Manager at PHA, deals with several difficult situations. "The Vineyard is a tough place to grow," he explains. "Deer, insect and disease pests, wind, a paucity of summer rainfall, and poor soils all present unique challenges in maintaining such a diverse collection of plants.

"Overall, the soil is very acidic," Clark continues, "impoverished and sandy with very little organic matter. Where we recently excavated for the shade house, the top six to eight inches was a reasonably good sandy loam that we

◄◄ Because it has beautiful exfoliating bark, a *Stewartia* tree is interesting in all seasons. There are several, including several Polly Hill introductions, at the arboretum in West Tisbury.

◄ In spring a row of *Fothergilla* blooms in the arboretum before many plants have broken dormancy.

► Near the Visitor Center at Polly Hill Arboretum, a magnolia (*Magnolia officinalis* X *M. tipetala* 'David') blossom attracts well-deserved attention.

▼ The pleached hornbeam arbor (*Carpinus betulus* var. *columnaris*) at Polly Hill was started in 1964. Each year the trees were trained, pruned, and sheared to create the tunnel, and pruning must be done annually to maintain this living arbor.

▼► In the Visitor Center at Polly Hill Arboretum a table displays cuttings from plants that are of interest. A map showing where those plants can be found is available as well.

▲ A wild turkey pays no attention to the beautiful bark on a *Stewartia monadelpha* as it strolls down the walk next to the arboretum's Visitor Center.

The Homestead Border at Polly Hill Arboretum was designed by Laura Coit. Because the plants chosen need to be able to survive with little supplemental water, Coit chose the native orange butterfly weed (*Asclepias tuberosa*), coneflowers (*Echinacea purpurea* 'Rubinstern'), lavender, prairie dropseed (*Sporobolus heterolepis*), and a Diabolo ninebark (*Physocarpus opulifolius* 'Monlo').

greedily stockpiled for use in the arboretum. Below that relatively good soil was coarse sand." Some parts of the property, such as the Homestead Border and Polly's Play Pen, have been mulched and top-dressed over the years, so the soil there is greatly improved. Other areas haven't had the same attention, however, and that is one of the staff's goals.

"As we further improve the soils," Clark explains, "we should see better growth, healthier plants, a more aesthetically pleasing landscape, and a more valuable scientific collection of plants. Central in our efforts to improve the soil is the incorporation of organic matter. This will aid in the soil's ability to hold moisture and nutrients, will buffer the pH, and create a healthier soil by encouraging more biological activity."

Improving the soil is one more duty necessary to keep the arboretum in good shape. Pruning, mowing, planting, weeding, and occasionally watering during a drought are just a few of the chores. Naturally, a garden that is open to the public needs to be kept attractive. But Thomas Clark hopes that visitors to Polly Hill remember that the ap-

pearance of the plants is not the entire focus of this garden.

"I think the most important thing for people to know is that the arboretum is so much more than just a pretty place," Clark says. "The trees and shrubs are to the arboretum what animals are to a zoo, or works of art are to a museum. They're the first things people see. But behind the scenes at all of these institutions there's much happening—research, conservation, education, and, of course, all that goes into managing and maintaining them. In the end, each individual who experiences the arboretum appreciates it in their own way, but knowing that there's more than meets the eye may enhance the experience."

Tim Boland says that the focus of this arboretum is on connecting plants with people. It is a mission of extreme importance because we all depend on plants so completely, yet we frequently treat them with ignorance or disregard. "It is our greatest challenge here at the arboretum and worldwide," Boland states, "with environmental crises all around, to convince people that living things must be protected, that we all must see the rich inherent value in nature and work *with* it, not against it."

▲ In the Homestead Border at Polly Hill the dark foliage of a Diabolo ninebark contrasts well with the gray-green leaves of the butterfly bush and the silver *Artemisia* 'Silver Mound' nearby.

◄ As the flowers on an oak-leaf hydrangea (*Hydrangea quercifolia*) age, they turn a rusty pink. These flowers catch the sun in front of the Visitor Center at Polly Hill Arboretum.

Chapter 3

DIFFICULTIES AND DILEMMAS

As Tom Clark, Collections and Grounds Manager at Polly Hill Arboretum, said, growing plants on Martha's Vineyard can be difficult. Deer, rabbits, and winter moth caterpillars eat the plants, and ticks spread diseases. Soil can be pure sand, compact clay, or rock-ridden, and the wind desiccates both plants and soil through the winter months. There may be long stretches of drought in the summer, and no spring at all. These are all ongoing concerns, and gardeners seldom find an absolute solution. "We can ameliorate some of these conditions," Clark says, "but they will remain as challenges."

Challenges, yes—complete deterrents, no. Gardeners are resourceful people, and islanders are doubly so. Through hard work, experimentation, and sometimes a bit of dumb luck, they persevere and find a way to cultivate what they want to grow.

Bambi or Beelzebub?

There is nothing sweeter than watching a spotted fawn follow its mother at the edge of the woods, and seeing a herd of deer leaping through the grasses is a beautiful sight. But when Bambi and his mother eat all the tulips and hosta, a gardener begins to have dark thoughts. And when the shrubbery is reduced to stubs in a single weekend, many a plant-loving pacifist begins to imagine fatal forms of revenge.

Short of shooting the animals during hunting season, however, islanders use many strategies for coping with deer. Some are more successful than others, and the methods used might need to be periodically changed.

Gardeners have tried a number of repellants for keeping

In the Grosses' Aquinnah garden plants grow in more sand than soil, and the off-ocean wind can be formidable. Plants such as American beach grass, sedum, and lavender tolerate the sharp drainage, sun, and wind.

deer at bay, including products and home remedies based on scent or taste. Those that repel deer with odors work best in warm weather, so the method that is effective in the summer may be less so in cold temperatures. The type of plants that need protection also determines the type of repellant that will be used. A product or home concoction that is suitable for ornamental plants may not be appropriate for fruit trees and vegetable gardens.

Some of the scent-based deterrents that gardeners have tried include human hair, highly perfumed soap, lion dung, and coyote urine. Although some report success using these methods, others say that they weren't effective at all. Many worry that coyote urine can't possibly be collected in a humane way, and where on the Vineyard does a person find *lion dung,* anyway?

Robert and Elise Elliston, who have planted a small vineyard in Chilmark, decided to try the scented soap cure when the deer began to browse on their grapevines. Robert read that Irish Spring soap would repel the deer, so he went to the store and purchased dozens of bars. After cutting each bar into three pieces, Robert drilled a hole in the center of each piece so that it could be nailed to the top of each vine stake. The deer came and ate anyway. "All of the bathrooms are still stocked with bars of Irish Spring," Robert laughs, "each with a hole in the center."

Gardeners find greater success with commercially prepared deer repellants. There many choices available in stores and online, including granular products that are sprinkled on the ground and liquids that are applied directly to the plants. There are concentrates that get mixed with water and those that come ready to spray. Some products combine a scent that deer don't like along with a taste

◄ Rocks in the soil can be one of the challenges faced by Vineyard farmers and gardeners. This pile is just a portion of the stones and boulders that Robert Elliston removed when preparing the soil to plant wine grapes.

▲ The tall plastic fence keeps deer out of this garden, and the chicken wire below prevents rabbits and other small animals from entering as well.

▲▶ The tall fencing at Whippoorwill Farm in West Tisbury prevents deer from grazing on the crops.

that they find repugnant, while others work by smell or taste alone.

Several of these products are labeled as being suitable for edible plants, and others are for ornamentals only. Although it seems obvious to advise that anyone buying a deer repellant should read the label before purchasing and using the product, it's surprising how many people forget to do this.

Island gardeners usually find repellents to be effective, but to be most helpful these products need to be used frequently and according to directions. A concentrate that is mixed using more water than recommended on the label, for example, will not be as effective as one that is prepared according to the instructions. Repellants need to be applied regularly through spring and summer because plants are constantly growing, and the new growth and flowers are appealing to deer. Abigail Higgins, a professional gardener on the island, reports that on some properties she needs to spray once a week during the summer.

With the necessity of such frequent applications, it's no wonder that many gardeners choose to purchase their deer repellants instead of making their own. But for those who want a less expensive, do-it-yourself approach, a home brew made of eggs, milk, water, and a little soap will work as well.

Red or black pepper can also be added to the mix, as can crushed garlic. Because this mix contains raw eggs, it should be used only on ornamental plants, never on fruit or vegetables.

The recipes vary, but basically you need two eggs per gallon of water. Add a cup of milk as well; deer are herbivores, so they do not like the taste or smell of animal products. Mix the pepper and garlic with a couple of cups of the water in a blender, strain this into the rest of the mixture, and pour the concoction into a sprayer. (Use a fine cloth to strain the mixture, or small pieces of pepper or garlic will clog the sprayer.) Then add a teaspoon of soap or spreader-sticker product, which can be found at your local garden center, after putting the mix in a sprayer. (Beware: adding

the soap to the blender will result in an amount of suds suitable for an *I Love Lucy* episode!)

In addition to applying repellants frequently, gardeners need to remember that the goal is not to stop the deer from damaging the plant, but to prevent the deer from trying it in the first place. Animals are creatures of habit, and once they get in the routine of eating a plant, it is harder to stop them than it would have been to prevent them from trying it originally.

If the routine spraying of all the plants in your landscape seems daunting, there are other ways to deal with deer. After the Irish Spring failed, Robert Elliston turned to man's best friend for help. Every evening the Ellistons would tie Lucy, the family dog, in the garden for the night.

◀ The stone garden shed at the end of Ben and Susanne Clark's garden was designed to break up the wall of deer fencing, in addition to holding gardening tools.

▶ The Higginses' vegetable garden is fenced to protect it from deer and other animals.

Although some canines would offer perfect protection in this situation, Lucy wasn't cut out to be a guard dog. "She would sleep on the job," Robert recalls, "so we had to put up a fence."

A permanent barrier is where many turn when all else fails, or if they decide that they don't want to fight Bambi in the first place. When Ben and Susanne Clark were planning to build their house in Chilmark, Susanne was aware that she needed to be concerned about deer. "I knew that I wouldn't have a garden unless I didn't have to battle the deer problem." So in the initial stages of their planning, Susanne designed an unobtrusive deer fence.

The Clarks' property is on a slope, and this works with the fence to deter deer from entering the garden. Deer are not at ease with jumping a barrier where there is a change of terrain; they may be able to jump in one direction but not the other, and it's more difficult to judge landings. In addition to the incline, Susanne installed terracing close enough to the fence that the animals perceive it as another barrier to an uncomplicated landing.

Susanne used tall wire fencing and designed two structures that make the barrier less obtrusive in the landscape. The first is a large arbor that allows the fence to be connected with the front of the house in a natural and attractive manner. The second is a stone saltbox building that was designed to look like a 1730s root cellar. The small stone house serves as a garden storage area, and it breaks up the fence on the front side of the garden. Looking as if it's been there for hundreds of years, the stone structure interrupts the fence line so that the area looks like a garden instead of a top-security detention center.

Deer fencing is also available in dark-colored metal and plastics that virtually disappear when strung through trees, and this is a good option for those who live on wooded properties. Such barriers are very tall and impossible for deer to jump over.

Electric fences don't usually need to be as tall as barrier fences, and some find that it works to put two electric wires on top of a regular four- or five-foot-tall fence. The electric wires are hooked to timers so that they stay on between evening and the early morning hours. There are also shock fences that are wireless. These are stakes that are loaded with a battery and bait. The scent lures the deer in, and when they touch their nose to sniff the bait, they receive an electrical shock. It sounds nasty, but the deer learn quickly never to touch one again, and they stay clear of the area.

That Rascally Rabbit

A fence that keeps out the deer may need to be modified to hold back rabbits. After the Ellisons fenced their vineyard against deer, they realized that small animals such as rabbits could still do a great deal of damage, so they added chicken wire around the bottom of the barrier.

Having solved her deer problem, Susanne Clark also had to deal with rabbits. In fact, they are one of her main challenges as a gardener. She points out that she can deal with the challenges of poor soil and exposed locations, but it is far more difficult to prevent animal damage.

Like deer, rabbits are herbivores, so the repellents that contain eggs or fish work for Thumper as well as Bambi. The same cautions pertain to dealing with rabbits: use eggs on ornamentals only, treat plants *before* they are nibbled on, and apply repellants regularly.

New Pests Bring New Problems

The introduction of new insect pests is as problematic on the Vineyard as it is in the rest of the Northeast. First it was hemlock woolly adelgid, then the red lily leaf beetle,

▶ Several problems were solved by the fencing and terraces around Rick and Roberta Gross's pool: the fence keeps animals and children away from the garden and pool, the terracing makes a steep grade usable, and the plants, designed by Steve Yaffee of Crosswater Landscapes, withstand the sun and wind of this exposed location.

▼ The chicken wire that keeps rabbits out of the garden becomes almost invisible next to the split-rail fence.

and now the winter moth caterpillar. It's a jungle out there! And just as the woolly adelgid has killed many hemlocks, winter moth larvae are stressing and killing deciduous trees.

The winter moth was introduced into this country from Europe, and it has been spreading throughout Massachusetts for at least five years. The male moth can be seen flying from around Thanksgiving well into December. Female moths cannot fly, and they wait for the males at the base of trees. Once the male has fertilized her eggs, the female climbs up the tree and deposits the eggs in cracks and crevices, or underneath lichen.

Winter moth caterpillars are particularly damaging because they hatch just at bud-break. As the bud swells, they worm their way into crevices of bud scales and bracts and begin feeding on the tiny bud. During cold springs, when the leaves don't develop quickly, the caterpillars can do substantial damage early on. They can eat the inside of developing flowers on blueberries and apple trees, so that by the normal bloom time there is nothing to pollinate.

Many types of trees are damaged by the winter moth, and maples, oaks, and apples can be especially hard-hit on the Vineyard. Shrubs such as blueberries and roses are also susceptible, and the caterpillars have even been seen eating perennials.

On trees that are small enough to spray, control is possible using Bt from bud break through mid-May. A product containing Spinosad is more effective when the caterpillars are larger, and it works on other caterpillars as well. This biorational compound is toxic to bees when it's wet, however, so plants in bloom should not be sprayed with Spinosad because it might hit foraging bees.

A shrub or tree that is healthy and strong may be able to put out a second growth of leaves after the winter moth is gone, but in some years the plant may also be attacked by cankerworms and gypsy moth caterpillars, which will leave it depleted. Other stresses such as drought can make a tree less able to leaf out a second time, so homeowners with defoliated plants should water them periodically if it doesn't rain.

Spinosad is also effective on the larvae of another relatively new pest, the red lily leaf beetle. The adult beetle is bright red with a black head, and the larvae resemble small piles of mud. They achieve this look by piling their own excrement on their backs for protection from predators. Although Spinosad does not kill the adult beetle, they are easy to hand-pick and smother in a can of cooking oil or squash between the fingers. Populations of red lily leaf beetles do seem to come and go, however, and gardeners report having a large population one year and a small amount of damage the next.

Ticked Off

Ticks are not a problem for plants, but because they spread an assortment of diseases, they can be big trouble for the gardener. Everyone is very familiar with the recommendations for wearing long pants in the garden, and tucking

those pants into socks or boots to keep ticks away from the body. A thorough inspection after working in the garden is also wise.

There may also be another solution to the problem. Wendy Forest, owner of the Seaside Daylily Farm in West Tisbury, has a flock of guinea hens that do a great job of controlling the ticks in the daylily fields. Wendy says that the guinea hens are not hers, but are semiwild. They spend the days moving from place to place, eating insects—including ticks. Wendy knows that they are effective because she never finds a tick on herself after working among the daylilies. But when she works in her vegetable garden, a fenced area where the guinea hens can't go, she frequently finds ticks on her body.

March, March, March

It is said that on Cape Cod, Nantucket, and Martha's Vineyard, we have January, February, March, March, March, June—and early June can be somewhat dicey. Certainly there are days in the spring when the sun is shining and the air is warm, but there just aren't very many of them.

The damp, chilly spring weather so typical on the Vineyard is certainly a problem for the gardener who wants to work in the landscape. But it's also difficult for many plants. Those who want to plant annuals early, for example, frequently find that the small impatiens that they put in the garden in May just sulk until mid-June, and that's the best-case scenario.

The cold off-ocean winds and the resulting cool soil are stressful for young plants. For many plants it is the temperature of the soil that signals the plant to grow. For this reason impatiens, zinnias, and tomatoes may fail to thrive through late May—or simply die. Other plants such as tropical flowers, eggplant, and basil do poorly when night temperatures drop below fifty degrees, and such readings are standard for a typical Vineyard spring evening.

A guinea hen eats hundreds of bugs every day, so some think that these birds are the perfect way to control ticks.

The solution to this problem is something that is often in short supply in spring: patience. After the winter months, everyone is desperately longing for warmer weather and looking forward to the summer ahead. Some mistakenly think that early planting will result in a flower-filled garden almost immediately, but in May there is no way to fool the plants into thinking that it's mid-July.

Alicia Lesnikowska, a botanically trained professional gardener, says that the prolonged chill dictates what she can and cannot plant. "I have given up planting anything except lettuce and beets until the third week in April," Alicia reports, "even though our last frost on Hines Point is usually in March. And I have to start dahlias and cannas indoors in April to get bloom by early July."

Where the Wind Blows

One of the reasons plants dry out so quickly on the island is the wind that keeps the Vineyard cool in the summer and warmer in the winter. The sea breeze may be a summer blessing for residents and tourists, but it is drying for plants. Plants lose moisture primarily through their leaves, and more moisture is lost in windy situations.

Winter winds are especially damaging to evergreens, because the moisture is not as easily replaced in frigid temperatures. In May it is common to see browned leaves on rhododendrons, for example. These leaves become obvious in the spring and early summer, but they were desiccated by the winter winds months before.

Because every property has areas that are more windy than others, this should be another factor when grouping plants in a garden. Alicia Lesnikowska says that some plants on her property can be seriously damaged by the winter winds. "In my own garden," she says, "which in terms of temperature is one of the warmest areas on the Vineyard, I have lost a tree peony and had camellias suffer." Although both of these plants are hardy in colder but more protected locations on the island, she knows that in her garden the wind makes it just too stressful for these varieties to survive.

Because shelter can make the difference between life and death for plants, there are ways to arrange a garden so that plants are protected. Wind-tolerant shrubs can be placed to shield other plants, for example, or a low stone wall constructed that will both break the air currents and absorb warming rays from the sun. Plants that are especially susceptible to damage by winter winds should be planted in sheltered locations. The proper placement of plants is preferable to wrapping trees and shrubs for the winter. Upholstery belongs on furniture, not on the landscaping!

Wind isn't the only challenge that island gardeners face during the winter. The fluctuations in temperatures can also be problematic for plants. "Our winters tend to have very warm spells in between the cold and the wind," Alicia says. This fluctuation is frequently harder on plants than months of constant cold. Woody plants such as lavender, butterfly bush, and heather can be severely damaged by what Alicia calls the island's "off-again on-again winter."

In some regions plants can be protected by an application of winter mulch, but this works best where temperatures stay consistently cold. Alicia says that she's reluctant to mulch very much because the mulch can form a soggy mat and encourage the rotting of plants underneath.

The bottom line is that whether protected in the winter or not, sometimes plants die in the cold season. "Every once in a while we have a winter that will kill all of the hydrangea canes back," Alicia says, "or the cold kills the buddleia back to the roots. Lavender is perhaps the most problematic. . . . I think the winter is usually responsible, and we lose some every year." That said, when asked what her biggest challenge as a professional gardener is, Alicia Lesnikowska answers that it isn't the weather, but "convincing people to invest in serious soil preparation instead of large plants." When it comes down to it, under all is the land, and attention to the soil should come first.

An Unsightly Septic System

Another problem that some island residents face is how to landscape an aboveground septic system. Such raised septic tanks are often mandated in low-lying areas, but they can be eyesores on otherwise attractive properties. These systems are usually made of concrete, which is a cold gray color. Common ways of making the concrete tanks more attractive include dyeing the mix a warmer color before it's poured and covering the walls with stone or a wooden lattice. Planting mixed shrub and perennial beds in front of the tank will soften the boxy shape as well.

My mother, Jan Albertson, was an interior designer in Wisconsin. Dealing with blots on the landscape, such as a raised septic tank, remind me that she used to say, "If you have a visual problem, *accentuate* it." This was precisely the approach the landscape designer Carly Look took on a property in Aquinnah. Instead of trying to hide the septic system, she designed it to be a bocce court. A low border of plants was placed around a grass court on top of the tank, and steps were constructed at the back, with taller peren-

nials and grasses placed in front of the tank to soften the perimeter.

Others plant the top of their raised systems with wildflowers or native grasses. A simple planting of one type of grass such as switchgrass (*Panicum virgatum*) is attractive and easier to care for than the common "wildflower meadow in a can" because weeds can be easily spotted and removed.

Insects, browsers, winds, and design dilemmas aside, the Vineyard is a wonderful place to garden, and some longtime residents don't find it difficult at all. "I don't think that there are many challenges," Elizabeth Luce of West Tisbury, says. "My soil is good, so there is every possibility of succeeding if you know what you're doing!"

▲ Shrub roses and ramblers flourish around this raised septic system.

▶▲ A stone wall and plantings by Carly Look have transformed the raised septic system at Mary Pat Thornton and Cormac McEnery's house into a beautiful garden.

▶ The top of this raised septic tank, designed by Carly Look, functions as a bocce court or a small garden room. Carly planted the borders with shrubs, grasses, and perennials so that the space is attractive from all viewpoints. What could have been an eyesore has been transformed into a terraced garden.

◀ Carly Look's approach to the Thornton-McEnery property seems in complete agreement with my mother's belief that a visual problem can be turned to an advantage. Instead of trying to cover the raised septic with evergreen shrubs or ivy, she faced the sides with attractive stone and planted gardens in front of and on top of the septic area that match beds on either side of the walkway. Grasses and other plants are repeated in all areas for continuity.

▶ Bocce balls wait on the side of the lawn under the Russian sage and fountain grass.

Chapter 4

LOCAL AND LOVELY

*I*t might seem that living on an island would foster an appreciation of the indigenous environment, and certainly this has happened on the Vineyard. But like the rest of the Northeast, indeed much of America, native landscapes can frequently be seen as a collection of unidentified weeds. In the quest for a beautiful garden, we've been encouraged to destroy all the wild plants, and we've paid no attention to the importance of biodiversity. Whether on Martha's Vineyard, Cape Cod, or elsewhere, it is common to find houses surrounded by a monoculture of turf grass and landscaping that might be seen in New York, Michigan, or Oregon.

People have gotten in the habit of choosing plants based on what they're familiar with, or what strikes them as pretty, and these plants are grouped according to what we like to *see* instead of what would make sense environmentally. Compounding the problem is the overuse of garden chemicals. For years gardeners have been trained to think that there is an easy solution-in-a-bottle for any problem, and this has dulled an appreciation for using the perfect plant for a given location. But if plants are given the conditions they prefer, there are fewer problems, or an acceptable level of damage, and much less need for human—or chemical—intervention.

Gardeners tend to forget that plants grow in communities in the wild, and these habitats support a wide range of organisms that live and work together. We have become so accustomed to choosing plants for the look of the foliage or color of the flowers that we fail to remember that native habitats function as a system where soil, plants, insects, animals, and microorganisms are interdependent.

It is easy to see why Carlos Montoya loves the native plants on Martha's Vineyard: the wetland visible from his yard is a feast of colors and textures all year.

Amid these prevailing customs and attitudes, however, grows a movement to better appreciate, preserve, and restore native habitats. Organizations such as the Nature Conservancy, the Sheriff's Meadow Foundation, the Vineyard Conservation Society, the MV Land Bank, and the Vineyard Open Land Foundation work to protect the indigenous flora and fauna and to educate the public about the unique wildlife and plants on the island.

Sand-Plain Grasslands, Heathlands, and Beaches

The native plant communities on the island are very distinctive. Martha's Vineyard is one of the few places where the sand-plain grassland ecosystem is found. This type of native grassland has evolved on sandy glacial deposits that were left after the advance of the Wisconsin

▲ Sometimes native plants are the most appropriate landscaping for oceanfront property. Bayberry, American beach grass, and beach plums all thrive in the sand close to the sea.

▼ Boneset, goldenrod, blazing star, and switchgrass are just a few of the beautiful plants that Carlos Montoya used on the slope by the Chilmark Free Public Library.

glacier, so it is found only in Long Island, Cape Cod, Nantucket, Martha's Vineyard, and surrounding small islands. In addition to the sandy soils, these areas all have a climate influenced by their proximity to the ocean, and the plants and animals that populate these regions have acclimated to the moderate temperatures and salt-laden, off-ocean winds.

As in the prairies of the Midwest, the key factor that maintains these grasslands is fire. The plants that thrive in a sand-plain grassland survive the periodic burning that prevents woody plants from slowly taking over. If the area isn't burned occasionally, trees and shrubs will need to be removed by cutting or by some other manner.

Typical plants found in the grasslands include little bluestem (*Schizachyrium scoparium*), common hairgrass (*Deschampsia flexuosa*), Indian grass (*Sorghastrum nutans*), and switchgrass (*Panicum virgatum*). These grasses grow in clumps, and other plants, such as several species of aster and goldenrod, are frequently seen growing in the spaces between them.

Heathlands also comprise plants that grow well in sand,

◄▲ Like many grasses, little bluestem catches the early morning and evening light, and it combines well with butterfly weed and other native perennials.

▲ This photo shows how beautiful the native joe-pye weed looks in a Vineyard garden

▼ The plantings along Carlos Montoya's driveway beautifully illustrate his point that native species should be planted in a community, or habitat, where they mix with each other.

▲ Planting groups of native plants in beds next to the lawn is a good way to make a visual transition from wild to tame in a landscape.

◄ The sickle-leaf golden aster (*Pityopsis falcata*) is an underappreciated native perennial that grows in the dry, sandy soil of pine barrens and sand-plain grasslands. Reaching eight to fifteen inches in height, this plant flowers from midsummer into September and combines well with goldenrod, switchgrass, and butterfly weed.

and most of the species that thrive here are low, woody shrubs, such as golden heather (*Hudsonia ericoides*), low-bush blueberry (*Vaccinium angustifolium*), and bayberry (*Myrica pensylvanica*).

Many people associate the beach rose (*Rosa rugosa*) with Cape and Vineyard beaches, but this plant is indigenous to eastern Asia, not Massachusetts. A few of the native plants that grow on the beaches of Martha's Vineyard include American beach grass (*Ammophila breviligulata*), beach pea (*Lathyrus japonicus*), seaside goldenrod (*Solidago sempervirens*), beach plum (*Prunus maritima*), and bearberry (*Arctostaphylos uva-ursi*). All these plants flourish in nitrogen-poor, sharply drained soil.

Woodland Natives

The vineyard woodland is home to pitch pine (*Pinus rigida*), American holly (*Ilex opaca*), and several oaks, including scrub (*Quercus ilicifolia*), white (*Q. alba*), and black (*Q. velutina*). In areas with a moister soil, black cherry (*Prunus serotina*), red maple (*Acer rubrum*), sassafras (*Sassafras albidum*), and tupelo (*Nyssa sylvatica*) thrive. Poison ivy (*Toxicodendron radicans*) will grow anywhere and everywhere.

There are flourishing understory and edge-of-the-woods plant communities where you'll find some of the aforementioned sand-plain plants, as well as species of shadberry

(*Amelanchier*), high-bush blueberry (*Vaccinium corymbosum*), inkberry holly (*Ilex glabra*), wintergreen (*Gautheria procumbens*), and bracken fern (*Pteridium aquilinum*), to name just a few.

Many people on the Vineyard celebrate the changing of the seasons by observing the changes in coastal and woodland environments, marking the flowering of protected natives like the lady's slipper (*Cypripedium acaule*), and enjoying the summer fragrance of sweet pepperbush (*Clethra alnifolia*)

▲ The beach plum (*Prunus maritima*) is an attractive, drought-tolerant shrub. Beautiful when covered with white, clustered flowers and when loaded with fruit, the plant is a nectar source for bees and food for wildlife. Beach plum fruit can vary in color from purple to red or yellow.

◄ Because of the leaf shape, sassafras trees (*Sassafras albidum*) are sometimes called mitten tree. Here the leaves of a young sassafras display gemlike drops of dew.

Butterfly weed and goldenrod provide brilliant summer color in Carlos Montoya's native landscape.

and swamp azalea (*Rhododendron viscosum*). The fall foliage color of island natives ranges from the subtle soft tan of the switchgrass to the brilliant red of the beetlebung trees, the name by which tupelos are known on the Vineyard.

Natives in the Landscape

Native plants can be used to protect the environments where they thrive and restore areas where invasive species or development has destroyed indigenous plant communities, but these plants are also of interest to gardeners. People are attracted to natives because they are less work, save money, support wildlife, and provide a healthier landscape.

When placed in the appropriate location, native plants tend to do well without the use of chemical fertilizers or pesticides. Regular watering is required only as the plants are getting established or in times of severe drought. In fact, some indigenous plants such as bearberry (*Arctostaphylos uva-ursi*) will suffer or die when placed in an area with frequent irrigation.

Because no synthetic pesticides or fertilizers are used to maintain native plantings, people are assured that these products are not running off into the public water supply or exposing children and pets to products that may be suspected carcinogens. And along with the reduction of landscape products comes a decrease in costs.

Gardeners also appreciate using plants that support a diversity of wildlife. Planting natural landscapes is one way to provide the environment necessary for the survival of songbirds and other creatures whose populations have dropped because of loss of habitat.

Just as there are many reasons to use native plants, there are also several approaches to including them in the landscape. Some people want a traditional lawn and flowerbeds but are willing to include natives within that conventional layout. Clumps of switchgrass, joe-pye weed, and inkberry might be planted along with other shrubs and perennials, for instance. Others like the customary plantings near the house but are willing to consider alternatives elsewhere on the property.

Carlos Montoya, a landscape designer and contractor whose specialty is native plants, says that it is sometimes possible to attract people to indigenous plants by suggesting diversity. "Most people want something colorful and fun around the house," Montoya says, "and if you concede that, then you can get them to buy into natives on the rest of the property."

In an effort to educate his customers about how certain native plants look, Carlos might take them on a field trip. "I have taken clients out into the wild just to show them a plant," Montoya says. "I might say, 'This is switchgrass,' and they'll respond, 'That's too tall,' or 'That's perfect!' It helps them to visualize it, and that's important."

Although many people picture a wildflower meadow as being filled with colorful blossoms, it is grasses that usually predominate, filling the area with motion and color.

Carlos Montoya has planted several native plants, including a sweet bay magnolia, joe-pye weed, and switchgrass, along this roadside in Aquinnah.

In addition to helping people know the growing habits of particular native plants, Carlos says that it's also necessary to understand that it isn't just one or two plants that are important, but a group of plants that grow together. Using the several species that make up the particular plant community of island natives is essential.

Kristen Henriksen, a professional gardener from Vineyard Haven who specializes in native plantings, also thinks education is indispensable. She finds that many people come to these plants with a great deal of misinformation or unrealistic desires. "Sometimes people think a plant is a native," Kristen explains, "because it's naturalized around the area. Queen Anne's lace is an example."

Having patience about how landscapes develop is also difficult. "Many people still have that expectation of instant gratification," Kristen states. "I may give them a mix of native annuals along with the perennials so that they have something that is special the first season."

One common belief about native plants is that they aren't very colorful. "You know, it's funny," Kristen says, "that I often hear that there's no color when you use native plants, and it's just not true! Early on you have the blue-eyed grass, then the butterfly weed, then liatris, followed by black-eyed Susans. And for those who are here in the fall, there are the beautiful asters. You can have a meadow filled with color progressing through the seasons."

Planting communities of indigenous plants may just be outside the average homeowner's experience. "I don't think that it occurs to people that it can be done," Carlos Montoya says. "Most people assume that if you want a meadow you go buy a pasture mix and put it down. They don't know people who install and they don't know how to maintain it.

Most nurseries don't have a native plant section, and people don't think of natives as a *habitat*. You have to think of how the plants grow together."

In the effort to educate more people about indigenous island environments, Montoya has installed such gardens in places where a large number of people will notice them.

▲ Carlos Montoya planted natives such as switchgrass in the beds around Cronig's up-island market. These plants often thrive in sandy, dry areas where other selections wouldn't do as well.

◄ Carlos Montoya believes that one way to increase appreciation for the beauty of native plants is to place them in public places where people can grow more familiar with their beauty.

► Carlos Montoya planted a small bog garden next to the parking lot of the Chilmark Free Public Library so that people will learn to appreciate native plants that grow well in wet soils. In mid- to late summer the large pink flowers on the swamp rose mallow (*Hibiscus moscheutos*) blend with the mauve blossoms of joe-pye weed (*Eupatorium purpureum*).

"The way around the lack of information about such plant communities," Montoya states, "is to do plantings at public spaces. They'll go to the up-island Cronig's Market, see something by the parking lot, and then ask 'What is this plant?'" Carlos, who has a love of sand-plain grasslands, installed the garden at Cronig's and another near the Chilmark library. He also planted a small bog garden alongside of the library's parking lot, so people can become more familiar with native plants for wetlands.

Both Kristen Henriksen and Carlos Montoya grow native plants, Kristen at Going Native Nursery on her property and Carlos on a friend's land in West Tisbury. Their growing methods are different, but their goal of furthering the use of indigenous plants is the same. "I mostly try to build habitat gardens," Kristen reports. "People come to me for xeriscapes and habitat gardens." Xeriscapes are gardens that are given no supplemental water once they are established.

Both started growing indigenous plants when they had customers ask for particular natives that were hard to find. "I ended up not being able to get the plants people wanted," Kristen explains, "so I started growing my own."

Carlos has developed a unique method of cultivating his plants. All the plants are started from seed, sown either in plug trays or directly into pots. Some seed is placed in the

Glorious Grasses

Ornamental grasses are great problem solvers in the garden. Many of them are drought-tolerant and not too picky about soil, and the deer don't eat them. Best of all, they add lovely textures, colors, and movement to a garden, and they can be used as groundcover in meadows or on slopes.

American beach grass (*Ammophila breviligulata*). Growing to a height of 2 to 3 feet, American beach grass is a native, spreading bunchgrass with multiple stems in a clump. The leaves are long and narrow, and in the summer they shine as they wave in the sunlight and sea breezes. This is one of the best grasses for planting in pure sand. *Ammophila breviligulata* can be planted in the fall or spring, and it needs irrigation only when the young plants are becoming established. Once plants have settled in, they will spread through underground stems called rhizomes.

Karl Foerster feather reed (*Calamagrostis arundinacea* 'Karl Foerster'). This grass is so prized by professional plant people that it was named the Perennial Plant of the Year in 2001. 'Karl Foerster' is the perfect grass when an upright element is needed in the garden. The grass itself grows about 3 feet high, and the feathery blooms reach up to 6 feet. This plant is also different from many ornamental grasses in that it blooms early in the season, not in the fall. It was named for the German nurseryman Karl Foerster, who was one of the people responsible for the resurgence of ornamental grasses in gardens. Plant this *Calamagrostis* in full or part sun.

Evergold sedge (*Carex hachioensis* 'Evergold'). This sedge prefers moist but well-drained soils in part shade. The blades are striped golden yellow, and in all but the harshest winter it is evergreen. 'Evergold' grows 12 to 16 inches tall and 2 to 3 feet in diameter, and it is attractive planted as a single specimen or in a group.

Sea oat grass (*Chasmanthium latifolium*). Native to eastern North America, sea oat grass is beautiful when placed en masse or as an individual plant. Growing to about 3 feet tall, this *Chasmanthium* is initially upright in form, but as the seeds become heavier, or after substantial rainfall, the plant bends toward the ground. This characteristic is useful for those who need a grass that gracefully droops over a pond or stone wall.

Sea oat grass foliage is a fresh green in the summer, but as the seeds age they turn a bluish-gray that is similar to the color of blue mophead hydrangea blossoms at the same time of year. Later in the fall the foliage and seeds turn copper-colored and then become tan or gray in the winter months.

Chasmanthium does self-seed, so gardeners who don't want to weed out young plants should remove the seeds before they scatter around the yard and garden. Since the seed heads dry well and are beautiful in dried arrangements, this isn't much of a problem. Sea oat grass prefers part shade and isn't as drought tolerant as other grasses.

Hakone grass (*Hakonechloa macra*). This clumping grass is low and graceful,

with arching, bamboolike foliage. Hakone grass grows well in part shade but will tolerate quite a bit of sun as long as the ground doesn't get too dry. Varieties such as 'All Gold' and 'Aureola' add bright yellow color to the garden from April until hard frost, but the Vineyard designer Carly Look is equally fond of the green *Hakonechloa macra*. Morning sun is the best exposure for gold varieties because they can turn brown on the edges in too much sun and lose the yellow coloring in too much shade.

Blue oat grass (*Helictotrichon sempervirens*). Grown for the striking blue of the foliage, blue oat grass grows about 18 inches tall and wide. When in bloom, the oatlike flowers and seeds droop above the foliage in early summer. This grass grows best in well-drained soil and full sun.

Japanese blood grass (*Imperata cylindrica* 'Rubra'), A short, spreading grass with an upright habit, this blood grass starts out green in the springtime and turns red as the summer progresses. Although it grows best in moist soils, it seems to tolerate drier conditions if given some shade in the hottest part of the day.

Occasionally this variety of *Imperata cylindrica* will revert to its all-green form, and if this happens, remove it immediately. 'Rubra' may spread, but it is not invasive, whereas the green form is usually very aggressive.

Japanese blood grass grows to about 18 inches tall and makes a good garden component or container plant.

Maiden grass hybrids (*Miscanthus*

Pots of switchgrass (*Panicum virgatum*) glow in the summer sun at Going Native Nursery.

sinensis named varieties). It is best to use named varieties of *M. sinensis* because the plain species is developing a reputation for prolific self-seeding. Varieties such as 'Morning Light', 'Yaku Jima', 'Rigoletto', 'Nippon', 'Adagio', and 'Variegatus' have not shown a tendency to spread. *Miscanthus* is a hardy grass that adapts to drier conditions once established. In general, this grass prefers moist but well-drained soils, and frequent splashing of water on the foliage can lead to rust diseases. Cut maiden grass down in February or March before the new shoots start to poke up through the old growth. If the clump dies out in the center, cut a chunk of living grass off the sides, replant, and throw the rest away.

Switchgrass (*Panicum virgatum*). Our native switchgrass is one of the most attractive ornamental grasses. There are several cultivars that have uniquely colored seed heads or foliage, and all turn a lovely golden tan in the fall. To see just how beautiful this grass is, go to Cronig's up-island market to see the clumps that were planted by Carlos Montoya.

Switchgrass grows in a wide range of soil types, and it is tolerant of part shade. Most varieties grow between 3 and 5 feet tall, depending on the amount of moisture available. *Panicum virgatum* is attractive planted singly or massed in a group.

Fountain grass (*Pennisetum alopecuroides*). One of the most reliable and beautiful of the ornamental grasses, fountain grass forms soft mounds of dark green foliage that is topped by foxtail plumes in late summer. *Pennisetum alopecuroides* (sometimes listed as *P. japonicum*) grows 3 feet tall and around 4 feet wide when in bloom. The cultivar 'Hameln' has finer-textured foliage and is a bit shorter, and 'Little Bunny' grows under a foot tall and wide. Fountain grass grows best in fertile, well-drained loam with regular, deep watering during times of drought. The grass is adaptable, however, and will tolerate sandy soil and some dry spells. *Pennisetum* does best in full sun, and it will withstand windy, exposed locations.

Little bluestem (*Schizachyrium scoparium*). This native grass grows in clumps that start out quite upright and get softer as the season progresses. Flower spikes grow up to 3 feet tall from July into the fall, and the seed heads catch the light, especially when the grass is located where it receives the evening sun. In the fall little bluestem takes on a bronze to orange color, so it's particularly effective when planted with fall-blooming asters or Nippon daisies. *Schizachyrium* is most attractive when planted in groups, and it can be used with other native plants in grassland meadow plantings. Little bluestem tolerates poor soil and drought, but it grows best if watered every two weeks or so during dry periods.

containers in the fall so that the seed can naturally scarify over the winter. Scarification is the breaking or softening of the outer seed coat that either speeds germination or allows it to take place. Seeds can be scarified by freezing and thawing or by being abraded by passing through an animal's digestive system.

All the seed in Montoya's nursery is sown by hand; it is then covered with a thin layer of the sandy potting mix so that the seed makes good contact with the soil and doesn't blow away. Too thick a layer can prevent germination, however, so care must be taken that there isn't too much or too little topdressing.

Carlos stresses how important it is to use locally started seed. "The *Sisyrinchium montanum* that grows on the island can look one way," he explains, using blue-eyed grass as an example, "and the same species from seed grown in the Midwest can look very different."

Kristen also stresses the importance of preserving the genetics of Vineyard natives, which can be difficult when the plants grow near off-island species that are similar but not quite the same. "The domestic *Liatris* can cross with

the native *Liatris* and might make a lesser strain," she explains. "It's mainly about trying to keep what native plants we have strong, and being careful about which plants cross-pollinate."

Growing natives can be tricky, however, because the demand isn't constant. One year there might be someone who is putting in a native planting and needs hundreds of plants, but the next year there are no sales at all. Unfortunately,

▲ Native plant experts point out that the New England blazing star that grows on Martha's Vineyard can be different from the same species that is growing elsewhere. For this reason, Carlos Montoya and others use only local seed when growing their plants.

At Carlos Montoya's nursery, he's developed a unique way to raise native plants. By removing the bottoms of the pots and sinking them into sand, he encourages deep root systems while controlling weed growth around the pots.

▶ With the help of Carol Knapp, a native plant gardener, Dawn Greeley is planting her slope with a variety of indigenous grasses and perennials. Dawn wants this field in front of her home to blend in with the surrounding landscape and to provide color and motion throughout the seasons.

most of these plants do better in the ground than in the pot, so ideally they should be planted when they are a year or two old and allowed to grow to maturity in place. And like all growing operations, a native nursery can experience winter kill, animal damage, and other unforeseen problems.

But despite these challenges, interest in using native plants seems to be growing on the Vineyard. This is especially true in Chilmark and Aquinnah, where people are concerned that their gardens blend in with the surrounding landscape. When Rick and Roberta Gross were ready to plant their property in Aquinnah, they wanted the natural environment of the dunes and the ocean to be the star of the show. *And* they wanted their garden to be easy to care for.

"I didn't want maintenance," Rick says. So they enlisted the help of Steve Yaffee of Crosswater Landscapes, and because the house was surrounded with sand, they planted the majority of the property with the native American beach grass. "We put in five thousand small plants," Rick laughs, "and it was like Hair Club for Men! when all the little plugs went in."

The whole idea, the Grosses say, was to have a landscape that celebrated being on Martha's Vineyard. "We live in Washington," Rick explains, "and the goal of being *here* is not to be *there*."

Similarly, when Dawn Greeley was planning the plantings around her Chilmark home, she enlisted the help of Carol Knapp. Although Dawn knew that she wanted a collection of dwarf conifers near the house, she wanted a natural transition between her garden and the environs. "I had to figure out how to get the two of these connected," Dawn says.

She and Carol came up with a plan to mix natives in and among the conifers around the house. "So I have shad in the garden because there's shad out there," Dawn explains, gesturing to the surrounding native woodland, "and there's *Clethra* in the garden because there's *Clethra* out there."

Dawn and Carol continue to work on the field in front of Dawn's house. "My plan for the field is rivers of color," Dawn remarks. "We're using goldenrod and blue-eyed grass and, for fall color, huckleberry. I call it painting with plants."

A Beetlebung by Any Other Name . . .

The trees that seem to be dancing at Beetlebung Corner in Chilmark are black tupelos (*Nyssa sylvatica*). Elsewhere, this native tree is known as a sour gum or pepperidge tree, but since colonial times it's been known as a beetlebung on Martha's Vineyard. The name comes from the way this hard wood was used at that time: bungs were corks, and the tupelo-wood mallets that hammered corks into barrels were called beetles.

Nyssa sylvatica grows best in moist, acidic soils, and it has been in cultivation since 1750. This tree makes a fine specimen plant when placed singly, and some lucky home-owners have one or more on their property. But when they're grouped as they are on Beetlebung Corner, the horizontal branching habit of the mature trees makes them seem like they are whirling dervishes, frozen in midtwirl.

In addition to its twisted shape, N. *sylvatica* is prized for its brilliant fall colors. The autumn foliage ranges from bright orange to reds and purples. These trees usually have either male or female flowers, and a wide variety of wildlife, including many birds, eat the female tree's fruit.

Because they have a taproot, beetlebung trees do not transplant well, but container-grown trees will survive the

▲ A large stand of joe-pye weed blooms beyond a rock wall in Chilmark.

◀ Little bluestem and switchgrass mix well in native plantings.

▲ Some think that intense autumn foliage color makes beetlebung trees (*Nyssa sylvatica*) most attractive, whereas others enjoy the whirling branches that are visible in the winter and early spring.

◄ The use of native plants in Vineyard landscapes is not without controversy. Some believe that only plants indigenous to Martha's Vineyard should be used, while others plant their landscapes with any North American natives. This narrow-leaf blue star (*Amsonia hubrechtii*) is native to the southeastern United States, but the qualities such as drought tolerance that make it a valuable plant there also make it useful for Vineyard gardens.

The sweet bay magnolia (*Magnolia virginiana*) often grows in a multistemmed form. Growing ten feet high and up, this lovely native tree has lemon-scented, creamy white flowers and red berries that are eaten by songbirds and other wildlife.

transfer from pot to ground very nicely. When planting a beetlebung, look for that wet area on the property: this is the perfect tree to grow in areas that don't drain well.

As a new Master Gardener, my introduction to beetlebung trees came in 1994. A woman brought a branch into the extension office, wanting us to identify her tree. Not being familiar with the leaf, I took it into the office of Bill Clark, the Extension Specialist. "Did she say that it has great fall color?" Bill asked me. "Yes," I answered, "she did." "And did she tell you where it's growing?" he queried. "She said it was growing near the edge of a lake," I replied. "It's a tupelo tree," Bill said, handing the branch back to me, "and when it turns bright red in the fall, *that's* when you go flounder fishing."

Chapter 5

ISLAND GROWN

Though one could argue that every plant on this island could be called "island grown," these two words have a particular significance on Martha's Vineyard. It is a phrase that has come to express the dedication to self-sufficiency, sustainability, and ecological awareness that islanders encourage and embrace. It sums up the desire to support each other, to have healthy food, and to lessen dependence on "the mainland."

Island-Grown Bouquets

One of the most visible of the island-grown offerings is the many bunches of cut flowers. In every town and at many crossroads there are bouquets for sale, often at self-serve booths by the side of the road. And unlike the standard blossoms at a florist's counter, these seasonal flowers are picked daily.

In a country where we have grown blasé about being able to buy strawberries twelve months a year and roses on any given day of the week, it is refreshing to value a plant that is *in season*. The cut flowers of Martha's Vineyard are perfect celebrations of the time of year, and they are appreciated not only for their beauty but also for their transitory availability.

Some cut-flower growers sell only from their roadside stands or the farmers' market, others supply local shops, and a few grow for special events or private clients. The location of the fields where the flowers are raised varies as well. A

Buckets of flowers wait to be sold at the West Tisbury farmers' market.

Fragrant cut lilies are available in late summer at Takemmy Farm on State Street in West Tisbury.

few cut-flower farmers, like Kenny DeBettencourt of Oak Bluffs, cultivate their crops within sight of the stand where they are sold. Others, like Mary Jackson, have a small plot that serves as the "storefront," but the primary growing is done elsewhere.

Beverly Bergeron has been growing cut flowers for ten years, and she says that she grows it all, from daisies to dahlias. Like Mary Jackson, who is her mother, she has a small plot near the road to help attract customers, but the majority of her flowers come from the cutting gardens around her home. Beverly says that from the outside, growing flowers for bouquets seems pretty straightforward, but as you continue to grow it gets more complicated. "The first season you're in business it seems easy," she says, "because you usually don't have the weeds or the bugs yet."

Teri Praskach, who has been growing and selling bouquets at the farmers' market for over sixteen years, agrees that the business is challenging. You have to keep deer, rabbits, and woodchucks out of your fields, and the insects and other small pests can do quite a bit of damage as well. "This year the slugs just *devoured* my annual phlox," Teri comments.

The business requires long hours during a very short

▲ White coneflower (*Echinacea*), coreopsis, and snapdragons fill one of Mary and Paul Jackson's beds with early-summer flowers for cutting.

▶ A happy display of sunflowers is a cheery sight at Beetlebung Farm in Chilmark.

◀ A third-generation islander, Kenny DeBettencourt has been growing flowers and vegetables for over thirty-five years. Kenny and his wife, Joann, raise their crops on two acres in Oak Bluffs, and the bright bouquets of zinnias are sold at their roadside stand off Wing Road. Kenny says that some customers are so delighted with the look of the flowers in the cans that they ask if they can take the can, too.

▼ Beverly Bergeron says that she grows flowers from daisies to dahlias. In late spring, when the annuals have just been planted, perennials such as these daisies provide flowers for the cans that display Beverly's bouquets.

◀ Flowers grow in the garden, along the fence, and up a trellis at Beverly Bergeron's cut-flower stand in Chilmark.

▶ On farmers' market day, Teri Praskach's truck is filled with beautiful flowers.

▼ Many vendors at the West Tisbury farmers' market display and sell produce from their trucks. Here colorful bouquets grown by Teri Praskach are held in cans, waiting to be sold.

season. "I usually get up between four and five A.M.," Teri explains, "because you have to cut before it gets hot." In addition to hoping for enough rain, but not *too* much rain, cut-flower growers need to offer the blossoms that their customers prefer. Praskach says that zinnias, snapdragons, and delphiniums are always popular with the flower-buying public. She sells predominantly mixed bouquets, but sometimes she will offer bunches of a single variety.

Besides growing the most well-liked types of flowers, the grower has to be aware of which colors are preferable. The hardest color to sell is red, Teri observes. "You can put some red zinnias in a bouquet with other bright colors, but unless it's Christmas or Valentine's Day, an all-red bouquet just doesn't sell."

At the self-serve flower stands a grower has all these challenges plus one other: people who don't put their money in the cash box. "There's always people that don't pay," Beverly Bergeron admits. "There's a bad apple in every bushel. I used to have an open box so that people could

make change, but that didn't work. I don't want to have to be here all the time being a flower cop, so I just have to hope that the honor system will live on here on the Vineyard."

Despite the difficulties, growers continue to cultivate flowers. Lili Williams, who supplies bunches of blooms to Fiddlehead Farm and to realtors, says that she worked as an estate manager for a while, but prefers the bouquet business. "I love growing and cutting," she says.

Beverly Bergeron clearly has a sense of humor about the venture. When asked why she chose to raise cut flowers, she answers, "The flowers don't talk back like the teenagers do."

And when questioned about the number of people who are selling bouquets on Martha's Vineyard, she smiles. "My husband and I were just laughing about that," Beverly says. "We were saying that in August it's like McDonald's—the same menu on every corner!"

Island-Grown Food

For an island that is a popular tourist destination and a vacation site for presidents and media personalities, it's pretty remarkable that the Vineyard has retained so much of its rural character. Local agriculture has not only been preserved on the island, but is also being encouraged and

▲ Signs at the Farm Institute's display at the farmers' market encourage shoppers to support local products.

◀ Fiddlehead Farm on State Road in West Tisbury is one of the many markets that feature locally raised produce. At the entry, colorful buckets hold equally colorful flowers raised by Lili Williams.

celebrated by the Slow Food movement that is taking root worldwide.

Carlo Petrini founded the Slow Food movement in Italy in 1986. According to the Web site of the American branch, www.slowfoodusa.org, Petrini started the organization in response to the opening of a McDonald's in Piazza di Spagna in Rome. The organization has clearly struck a chord with people everywhere: there are now chapters in fifty countries around the world, including one on Martha's Vineyard.

The mission of the Slow Food organization suits Vine-yard residents in that the association encourages a system that produces food of high quality and taste using environmentally sustainable methods. Seeing the cultural, societal, health, and economic benefits of regional food production, this movement strives to create a food system that is "good, clean, and fair."

The Martha's Vineyard chapter of this organization has monthly meetings, special events, and projects to promote growing, cooking, and eating of locally grown foods. Its members advocate for the preservation and growth of small farms and local fisheries and encourage islanders to grow their own food. They also support island restaurants that serve locally raised food.

Melinda Rabbitt DeFeo, a Martha's Vineyard Slow Food member, says that the group works to support local agriculture in several ways. "We do things like have community potlucks and discussions for our members," she explains. "We're having a tomato tasting this year that will highlight heirloom vegetables, and we're working to help get local foods into the Vineyard schools."

In addition to the Slow Food association, the island has two similar groups that are specific to the area: the Martha's Vineyard Agricultural Society and the Island Grown Initiative. The Agricultural Society was established in 1859 with the stated purpose of promoting agriculture, horticulture, land conservation, and youth activities. The Island Grown Initiative works to raise consumer awareness about the importance of locally grown food, as well as to support local farmers.

When I remark that it seems that the Vineyard is ahead of the rest of the Northeast when it comes to advocating for local agriculture, Melinda DeFeo agrees. "We feel that way. Our logo has a wave on it, and we like to think that we're on the front of the wave of the interest in local foods. Within the last five years it's just exploded . . . not just the local community, but people who are coming from other places are starting to catch the bug. It's really exciting."

Rebecca Gilbert, one of the members of the Island Grown Initiative, thinks that the Vineyard is unique in many ways. Rebecca and her husband, Randy Ben David, own Native Earth Teaching Farm in Chilmark, and Rebecca says that they are lucky to have such a wonderful community of local farmers. "No one farmer can have everything," she explains, "and by being a part of the community, you can exchange things. The island is a rich community that way. Our other big advantage is that we have the visitors who don't come from farming communities, but they appreciate things like fresh vegetables. In these ways it's ideal for that flowering of interest in locally grown food to happen here."

Rebecca has found that the interest on the part of island

visitors and residents does not come simply out of love for full-flavored foods, however. "A lot of our customers have problems with their health or their children's health," she reports, "and these problems are exacerbated by chemicals in their food. I've heard some sad stories. But on the positive side, locally grown food is morally satisfying and it tastes much better. I myself am spoiled by the flavor!"

▲ The stand at Native Earth Teaching Farm in Chilmark has a chalkboard listing instructions and upcoming events, along with the seasonal produce for sale.

▼ At the Native Earth Teaching Farm there are plots available for rent. These allotments can be planted with flowers, vegetables, or anything that the renter desires, and Rebecca Gilbert says that they've seen *people* grow as a result of tending these gardens.

Rebecca stresses that the interest in locally grown food isn't new to the Vineyard. "There's always been a strong agricultural tradition on the island among people living here," she says. "When I go to my fourth- and fifth-generation islander in-laws', the food that you bring that is appreciated most is the food you've raised and harvested, or the seafood you've caught."

In the past, Rebecca thinks, it might have been difficult for tourists to find locally grown foods. "I think that when you go somewhere interesting, one of the first questions you should ask is 'What good food do you have here?' There is a tradition of that on the island," she continues, "but people who only visit a short time may not make those connections to local food. Now it's easier to find that information —it's on the Internet and on the Island Grown Initiative map."

The map Rebecca refers to was printed by the Island Grown Initiative (IGI, www.islandgrown.com) so that both residents and visitors would have an easier time finding island-grown produce. It raises awareness about the types and amount of agriculture on the island and helps the farmers advertise what they do. The organization is working on other ways to assist local farmers as well. The IGI plans to create a blog where farm-ers can post what will be available from their farms, so that restaurants and individuals can see what crops are offered and plan their menus accordingly.

"We've also purchased a chicken processing unit that will be approved so that farmers can sell local chickens off their farms," Melinda DeFeo says. Because there are many regulations that have to be met for killing and selling animals, most farmers can't supply the equipment and trained personnel to run it. The IGI will be sure that the processing equipment meets all state laws, and it will be leased out to a local landscaping company. This will help the landscapers employ their crews during the slow season, and it will give the local farmers what they need to take locally raised chickens directly from farm to market. "Our goal is to have locally grown birds in our supermarkets in less than five years," Melinda states.

In addition, the Island Grown Initiative is working to provide a map that would show farmers where there is available agricultural land on the island. "Farmers are so busy that they often don't have time to do their own marketing schemes." Melinda explains, "and they may not have time to figure out how to take advantage of something else that's out there."

Appreciation for the flavor, purity, and freshness of island-grown food, and even the willingness to pay higher prices for it, may not be enough to preserve island agriculture on its own. "It's hard to make a living at this," Rebecca Gilbert admits. "The food may seem expensive to our customers, but we don't make enough to support ourselves. I want to be able to look a young person in the eye and say, 'You should be doing this!' But there are few farmers on this island who are totally supported by their farming. I think that in the future if people want locally grown food, they're going to have to supply more help. The community will have to go further than just buying our vegetables."

Agricultural Education

One of the ways to spread the appreciation of local food and farming is through agricultural education, and perhaps the best place to start is with children. The Farm Institute was started in 2000 with the mission of connecting the community, and specifically the children of Martha's Vineyard, with the culture of agriculture. The Farm Institute recently moved to Katama Farm, a two-hundred-year-old former dairy that the Town of Edgartown had the foresight to purchase and preserve in 1979.

The Farm Institute's Web site explains that the organization "serves as a steward of the rich traditions of Vineyard farming and strives to become a place at the center of the community where children, families and generations can once again be engaged with the land. Our belief is that just about everything a child learns—values, work ethic, teamwork, commitment to community, caring for the land, even the 3-R's—are experienced on the farm."

"We have a lot of room and a lot of potential," states Melinda DeFeo, the Education Program Manager. Summer

▲ Colorful signs on the Farm Institute's barn remind people to return their tools to the proper place, *and* to celebrate the garden.

▼ From the hayloft at the Farm Institute you have a good view of the compost pile and the Friendship Garden.

day camp programs draw island residents and summer visitors. There are "farmer-in-training" classes and experiences in all aspects of agriculture from seed starting to milking and barn repair. "In off-season we run after-school programs and field trips through the schools," Melinda explains, "and we take what the teacher is teaching and apply that subject to the farm."

Children who attend the summer camp plant and harvest vegetables and learn how to cook or preserve them. Melinda describes how she teaches the younger kids to keep the weeds from overwhelming the garden. She takes them into the farm's Friendship Garden and explains that every plant that's growing in that space is competing for the same resources. "This soil only has so much moisture and nutrients that help our vegetables to grow, and these weeds are using those up," Melinda tells the children. "What do you think we should do?" "We have to pull them up!" the kids respond. "Come on! We have to weed!"

Melinda reports that parents frequently ask about the aspects of farm life that their children have talked about at

Curious ducks come to inspect visitors to the Friendship Garden at the Farm Institute in Katama.

Behind the rabbit hutches at the Farm Institute is a world map circle garden where plants form continents and children can learn geography *and* farming.

home. "By teaching the kids," she says, "we get the opportunity to engage the adults—instead of trickle-down it's trickle-up."

The Farm Institute also offers workshops for adults in cooking and gardening skills. "We have some great caterers on the island," Melinda observes, "and they all want to teach. We want to do more of that traditional art of preparing and preserving food. We're trying to raise money for a bunkhouse with a kitchen attached to that so we'd have a kitchen that would accommodate more people."

There is also space on the Katama Farm for a community garden. At present there are thirty plots, and there is room to expand these allotments if needed. Included in the rental fee is an eight-by-ten plot, all the necessary tools, many seeds, and monthly information sessions when needed. Those who rent a space grow their choice of vegetables, flowers, and herbs.

In 2007 the Farm Institute also attracted people to the farm with a seven-acre corn maze. This has proven to be a good way to generate a bit of income, introduce people to the farm, and provide a family activity that appeals to all ages. The maze benefits the farm in other ways as well, according to Melinda DeFeo. "We do grow feed corn in our maze," she explains, "and we have a corn and wood pellet stove, so after the harvest we'll be heating the building with something we've grown here."

The Farm Institute isn't the only place where children and adults can experience the agricultural life. On the other side of the island, Rebecca Gilbert and Randy Ben David have opened their farm to the public. Rebecca says that they started the Native Earth Teaching Farm because they saw a need to connect people with the source of their food. "We met so many people who didn't know the difference between a chicken and a duck," Rebecca recalls. "The agricultural fair is good, but not everyone can get there, and it doesn't show animals and plants in a farm setting."

Native Earth Teaching Farm is open to the public three days a week. "The other four days we try to do the farming and run errands. There is so much to do on the farm, and we have many good ideas, but time is the limiting factor." On the days that they are open, there are signs on many pens, and children can do the "chore of the day."

As I sat with Rebecca on the shady porch of the Native Earth Teaching Farm's produce stand, a father came in with two daughters who were eager to do some of the farm chores. After getting directions from Rebecca, they enthusiastically loaded a bale of hay into a wheelbarrow and pushed it over to feed the goats. "Just throw the hay over the fence to the two billy goats," Rebecca told them, "but you can open the gate and go in with the mamma and her kids."

Gilbert explained that some people come to dig their own potatoes or pull garlic, and there are a number of different types of poultry and small animals for children to feed. "In the winter we're open one morning a week," Rebecca says. "We call it 'Toddler Time,' but you don't have to have a toddler to come—it's really open to the public. We also do special visits that are tailored to a group or specific situation. For example, this summer some Girl Scouts are coming to study the three sisters garden."

Like the Farm Institute, the Native Earth Teaching Farm also has garden plots where people can lease growing space. There are eight plots that get rented to people who may not have the space for a vegetable garden, or enough sun to plant on their own property. Rebecca and Randy till this area in the spring, and then those who sign up can plant what they want there. "Everyone grows things that they like," she says.

Rebecca and Randy cultivate five of their total of twenty-five acres, and they sell vegetables, small fruits, eggs, and flowers from the farm stand at the front of the property. But although their produce is for sale, their real mission is to inspire others to raise their own.

"We hope to persuade more people to grow food at home," Rebecca explains. "Most businesses would rather be the only one doing what they do, and have the entire market to themselves, but our goal is to *encourage* people to do what we do."

Island-Grown Marketing

The markets and food shops of Martha's Vineyard all carry some amount of island-grown produce, and one, Fiddlehead Farm, has a mission to stock as much locally grown and harvested food as possible. Some islanders do their "marketing" with a stop at Whippoorwill Farm to pick up their weekly allotment of fresh produce. Andrew Woodruff has organized Whippoorwill following the concept of Community Supported Agriculture (CSA), whereby people purchase shares of the food that the farm grows annually.

Andrew started the farm in 1981 as part of an agriculture internship through the University of Massachusetts at Amherst. He now owns eight acres on Old County Road, and about two acres are planted. He started the CSA in the early 1990s and now leases other crop land in ad-

Everywhere you turn at the West Tisbury farmers' market, there are bouquets of colorful annuals. The market is held on Wednesday and Saturday mornings at the Grange Hall on State Road.

▲ Sunflowers, cosmos, and potatoes are just a few of the locally grown goodies from Tiasquam Brook Farm.

▼ Rows of freshly picked lettuce are every bit as pretty as the flowers at the farmers' market.

dition to using his own. CSA members pay a flat fee at the beginning of the year and are then able to pick up a weekly share of the harvest during the growing season.

Whippoorwill Farm also sells produce at the weekly West Tisbury farmers' market outside the Grange Hall on State Road. Local farmers and producers of other island-grown goods sell their wares from under tents, tables out in the open, boards placed across wooden sawhorses, and the back of trucks. For many years the farmers' market was open only on Saturday mornings, but recently Wednesday mornings were added during the summer.

Susan Silva, one of the founders of the market, says that it was started in the 1970s. "I just remember that Ron and I'd had a roadside stand for a number of years and it just did us in," Silva says. "We traveled around and went to other

▲ It's a good thing that I snapped this photo of Ethel and Ralph Sherman's squash early in the morning—by the time I walked back through the farmers' market a second time, these island-grown beauties were gone.

◀ The North Tabor Farm stand at the farmers' market is always well stocked and tended. On the morning this photograph was taken, a summer worker, Emily Palmer, had help from her mother, Linda Palmer, who was visiting on the Vineyard.

▼ Squash that are so fresh that they still have flowers attached are displayed with tomatoes, herbs, and other garden produce at the Stannard Farms stand at the farmers' market.

farmers' markets in the state, and thought that it would be good for local people to be able to sell their produce." The Silvas got together with others and the West Tisbury farmers' market was born.

The farmers' market has grown since those early days, and it is run by an organization of the people who participate. There is an annual meeting to determine rules and procedures. Vendors need to have a license from the town, and they have assigned spaces where they set up their tents, tables, and trucks.

Perhaps because it is such a new addition to the schedule, the Wednesday market is quieter, with fewer vendors and buyers. Saturdays are bustling, as eager buyers snatch up produce and flowers, and lines form for the homemade egg rolls and baked goods.

In addition to the fresh offerings, other island-grown items are displayed at the West Tisbury farmers' market. Lavender sachets, jars of jams and jellies, and sweaters knit from island-raised sheep fill some stalls, while others offer herbs and herbal products.

Holly Bellebuono is an herbalist who sells salves, tinctures, and other herbal cosmetics and treatments from her

booth at the farmers' market. Holly uses locally grown herbs in her products, and her interest in herbs comes from several directions. Holly finds herbs fascinating from scientific, historical, practical, *and* mystical viewpoints, and she enjoys sharing her knowledge through workshops and medicinal herb identification walks.

▶ Conservation lands and walking trails are filled with opportunities to learn about plants. Holly Bellebuono, an herbalist on the Vineyard, takes people on herb walks, during which she teaches people to identify plants that are now, or have traditionally been, used for eating, healing, and cosmetics.

▼ Island-grown salves, tinctures, and other herbal products are displayed on Holly Bellebuono's table at the farmers' market in West Tisbury.

Island-Grown Grapes

Traveling on State Road in West Tisbury, you may have seen the sign directing you toward Chicama Vineyards. This winery was founded in 1971 by George and Catherine Mathiesen, and it is still run by three generations of the Mathiesen family. Growing on the eleven-acre vineyard are shiraz, viognier and chardonnay grapes, and a few of the wines produced at Chicama have Vineyard-appropriate names such as Oceanus and Hurricane Chardonnay.

But Chicama isn't the only vineyard on the island. Others are also growing the crop that is, in name at any rate, appropriate to this region: a vineyard on the Vineyard, so to speak. In 2001 Robert and Elise Elliston started thinking about planting one in Chilmark.

"Well, it all started when our daughter graduated from college and came back for the summer," Robert remembers.

◀ The green nets are hung over the vines at Chicama Vineyards just before the grapes ripen enough to become desirable to the birds.

▼ Colorful annuals mark the entry to the tasting room at Chicama Vineyards in West Tisbury.

"One of the jobs she had was at a wines and spirits store. I was out mowing the wild grapevines down during the day, and she would come home saying that people were asking for local wines and she didn't have much to give them. We'd been making jelly from the wild grapes, and I started noticing that the jars of jelly were disappearing—our daughter was taking jars of jelly to the store and selling them! People wanted something from the island to take home."

That winter Robert bought a book about winemaking, and after reading it, he ordered twelve vines from one of the suppliers listed in the resource section. Remembering how well the wild grapes grew on his property, he decided that wine grapes might thrive as well. "I picked a nice sunny spot and planted them," Robert recalls.

So began a journey that took the Ellistons to California to see what winemaking was like in Napa. Robert says that they began buying and reading more and more books about growing grapes for making wine, and in 2004 they toured vineyards in France. "At that time we said that we have to

Robert and Elise Elliston's dream of having a vineyard on Martha's Vineyard is taking root in back of their home in Chilmark. To grow a large crop on a small piece of land, they have used an old French method of planting grapes one meter apart.

make a decision about whether we are doing this or not," Elise recalls. While in France they saw one area that the Ellistons thought looked a great deal like Menemsha, the coastal town to the north of where the Ellistons live. They visited a vineyard where the vines were planted one meter from each other in all directions and were trimmed to one meter high. Planted in this way, you can get one thousand vines in a quarter acre. Although most American vineyards don't use this method, the Ellistons were intrigued. "We don't have a lot of land," Robert says, "so that was the strategy that we wanted to pursue."

"Most vineyards space things to get a tractor down the rows—but I'm a hard head," Robert admits with a grin. To prepare the soil, Elliston used a backhoe to make trenches that were six feet deep for each row. "I removed about two hundred tons of stone," he reports, "but I wanted to *really* break the soil up." Loosening the soil down so far makes it easier for the roots to get quickly established and promotes a deep root system. Grapes are capable of forming very deep roots when growing conditions are right.

The land behind the Ellistons' had been a meadow for at

least a hundred years, so Robert wanted to find out what was needed to turn it into a vineyard. After sending soil samples to two labs, they received very specific recommendations for organic soil amendments that would help the grapes grow. Robert was then ready to replace the soil, adding in the soil amendments a layer at a time. "It took months," he says, "but when it was finished, we were ready to place stakes where the vines would go."

One thousand vines were planted by hand with the help of family, friends, and neighbors. Fences went up to protect the young vines from deer, rabbits, and other hungry critters, and the plants began to grow.

"By the third season we had to decide how we were going to trellis the vines," Elise says. "We wanted to put in something that we could use forever and ever. We had some locust, and that makes the best posts, so we decided to use that." Locust has a reputation for longevity in the environment because it is very slow to rot. "The old-timers say that locust posts will last one year longer than concrete," Robert adds.

The Ellistons put up the lower level of the trellising, and once the plants grow they'll add a second tier to bring the vines to a meter high. The vines will produce Cabernet grapes, which are a difficult grape to ripen in the Northeast because they take longer than others, but the Ellistons hope that the south-facing slope the vines are on will be a suitable microclimate for this variety. "It's going to be a challenge," Robert admits, but he says it with a smile and a light in his eye that makes you believe that those grapes will ripen just fine.

Because their property is near the old Brick Factory in Chilmark, they have a dream to build a winery that is made out of brick. "There were three island barns that were built from the bricks that were the rejects from the brickworks," Robert says, "and two are still standing." A brick building for Chilmark winemaking would be appropriate, the Ellistons think.

Just when the winery will be constructed, the Ellistons don't yet know, but the vines should bear their first fruit in 2008. Maybe it's Robert's joy and enthusiasm, or maybe it's standing on the sun-filled slope and looking at those young vines, but somehow it all makes a person want to see it come to fruition. Robert sums it up this way: "We just have a dream, that's all."

Island-Grown Perennials

Wendy Forest also had a vision that brought her island-grown business into being. But her aspiration was about environmentally sound plant and flower production, not winemaking. Wendy's dream began with a summer job in a greenhouse. She had graduated from college with a degree in environmental design, and although she enjoyed working with the greenhouse plants that summer, she kept thinking that there had to be a better way to run a horticultural business.

"I wasn't comfortable with all the plastics and chemicals that we used," Wendy says. "I wanted to design a system for

Knowing how important beneficial insects are in keeping habitats in balance, Wendy Forest does not mow a large area on the Seaside Daylily Farm. The plants and flowers here attract the "good bugs" and provide a place for them to overwinter.

▲ During midsummer hundreds of daylilies come into bloom at the Seaside Daylily Farm in West Tisbury. The farm is open only a few selected days a week, but you can always visit online at www.seasidedaylily.com.

▶ Rows of daylilies surround a shady arbor at the Seaside Daylily Farm. Wendy Forest chose daylilies as her crop because they can be grown without plastic pots, can be shipped bare-root, and are not prone to insect damage or diseases.

growing plants that worked *with* nature, and at the same time I wanted to create a wholesome, peaceful life for myself."

Wendy is clearly as thoughtful as she is committed to an environmentally friendly growing operation. Those who visit the Seaside Daylily Farm on the few days it is open to the public will be taken not only with the beautiful flowers, but also with the planning that has gone into the business. Phil and Wendy Forest are dedicated to growing with care.

The choice of the daylily was the first deliberate decision that Wendy made. She chose this plant because it has a wide variety of colors, sizes, and bloom times. Daylilies are very dependable and don't require much maintenance as they grow, and because they have thick, tuberous roots they can easily be shipped bare-root, so that no plastic pots are needed. This perennial can also be propagated without a greenhouse, so the Forests wouldn't need to burn fuel to heat growing spaces.

At the Seaside Daylily Farm, the product being sold is

considered to be a part of the ecosystem of the farm. The plants are grown organically, and the electricity for the farm comes from solar panels. Wendy encourages beneficial insects by leaving some areas wild, and the paths between the daylily beds are filled with fescue to prevent erosion. When the grass is mowed, the clippings get blown onto the daylilies, and this further amends the soil.

A drip irrigation system deposits water at the base of the plants, not on the paths or surrounding vegetation. This method of watering also ensures that there is little to no water lost through evaporation. Horse manure from a

The care and thought that go into the business add to its appeal, and the daylilies that the Forests grow are beautiful. Dug and packed the same day that an order comes in, these plants are truly farm-fresh when they are sent out. Wendy reports that although they ship daylilies throughout the United States, their focus is on the northeastern states.

The Seaside Daylily Farm offers all types of *Hemerocallis*, but the Forests also grow and sell some daylilies that were hybridized on Martha's Vineyard. These plants were named for the special features of the island, and the entire group is called the "Seaside Treasures Collection." From this special group of plants to the sustainable growing and selling practices, the Forests' company exemplifies the qualities that people hope for in a business that is island grown.

Island-Grown Art

When reading or hearing those two words—*island grown*—most people think about plants. Be they bouquets of fresh flowers, assorted vegetables or fruit, or even grapes for wine, it's the plants that come to mind. But growing in Vineyard Haven is a small, colorful garden that supplies an artist with the means to create island-grown *art*.

Peggy Turner Zablotny says that like a garden, her pressed-flower artwork just evolved. "It was just one of those fluky things," Peggy says. "I bought a tiny flower press that would compress one flower at a time. Then I made a bunch of presses and started doing many different types of flowers." The first actual print that was made from her pressed flowers was done for a wedding invitation, and this started Peggy down a path that led to the colorful and fascinating prints made from her pressed-flower collages.

"I just tripped across the giclée printing process," Peggy explains. "We found a guy in Maine who did the process and when he saw my work he said, 'You'd just be amazed if you blew this up.'" The detail that can be seen when Peggy's collages are enlarged is indeed remarkable. The veins in a flower, subtle colors or shading, a hairy surface, and textures that are normally not seen are now fascinatingly visible. And like all collage work, the whole is greater than the sum of the parts. It is Peggy Zablotny's composition, not the

neighbor's farm is used to improve the soil, and the plants are packed for shipping in recycled boxes.

The Forests' daylily farm is open to the public during very limited hours and by appointment, and this too was a deliberate, thoughtful decision. Most of the sales come from orders placed through their Web site, www.seasideday lily.com. This keeps their property peaceful and ensures that there isn't a great deal of traffic to bother the neighbors. "We want a fairly quiet, rural lifestyle," Wendy says. Web site sales also mean less use of paper and other resources to print catalogs.

▲ Combining all colors of annuals, perennials, and shrubs, Peggy Zablotny has created an oasis in her Vineyard Haven backyard.

▶ Bright yellow sunflowers against a blue sky are the essence of summer. Peggy Zablotny grows sunflowers, and many other annuals and perennials, in her large flower garden.

▶▶ As an artist, Peggy Zablotny is not afraid of bright colors. She and her husband, Stephen, are designers who live in Vineyard Haven, and Peggy uses plants from her garden to make giclée prints of her delightful pressed-flower collages.

individual pressed flowers or the technology used to enlarge them, that makes these prints extraordinary.

Peggy gathers foliage and flowers from her garden, from the gardens of friends, and from other locations when she travels. The plants are placed in a flower press and left until they are flat and dry. She can then use the small pieces to create a composition, and once the arrangement is to her liking, it's held under glass and photographed as quickly as possible. Although the inks used in the giclée print will last a very, very long time, the colors in the original collage will fade quickly.

Peggy's always on the lookout for new types of plants, and until she tries pressing them she never knows how each will work. "Sometimes new flowers press terribly and sometimes they press well," she says. "It's a learning process, but it should be fun at the same time."

That delight can be seen in Peggy's garden. This is no "pastels only" garden: orange and magenta cosmos surround brilliant yellow sunflowers, and the crisp white petals of a perennial hibiscus look like freshly starched linen in the sun. There is color and pattern everywhere in this garden. "I think about my garden in the same way I think about my art," Peggy explains. "I was wishing I could fly above it—if I hovered over the garden it might look like my artwork."

Peggy Turner Zablotny creates her artwork from pressed leaves and flowers, many of which come from her garden. The piece above is called *Habitat for a Dragonfly* and the one below is *Challenge . . . The Journey to Here and Now*. Photographs are by Peggy Zablotny; used with permission of the artist.

Chapter 6

JULY AND AUGUST

There are, of course, people who savor their gardens twelve months of the year. Whether they live on Martha's Vineyard or elsewhere, the landscape brings pleasure in warm and cold weather. From the first spring bulbs and early flowering trees to the frost that lines the edges of holly foliage in early winter, there is much to relish in the passing of the seasons and the changes that this brings to the landscape.

But on the Vineyard July and August reign supreme. Summer is the season when there are the most people on the island, and although many moan about the traffic, it makes sense that people enjoy the island at this time of year. They come for the sea breeze, for the ocean, for the island's annual events, and to enjoy the pastoral beauty— and many come to take pleasure in the gardens.

There is an abundance of plants to appreciate in the height of the summer. In early July the gray-shingled and white-painted houses are adorned with pink roses and blue hydrangeas. Later in the month other shrubs and perennials join the still-blue hydrangeas, and the bright orange and yellow of the daylilies mix with butterfly bush and fragrant lavender. August is in flower with black-eyed Susans, purple coneflower, hardy hibiscus, rose of Sharon, and peegee hydrangeas, to name just a few. In July and August the annuals are also at their peak. Bright blue salvias, zinnias, geraniums, impatiens, petunias, and more produce colorful displays all over the island.

It seems that most Vineyard gardeners like landscapes in which annuals, perennials, shrubs, grasses, and trees are

The artist Lew French built the stone walls, buildings, and structures on this property, and Carly Look designed the gardens. Lew's stonework, Carly's choice and placement of plants, and the maintenance done by Carly's crew of gardeners assure that this garden remains a striking environment all summer.

▲ A mix of berries and flowers make a colorful display designed by Carly Look. American cranberry bush (*Viburnum trilobum*), butterfly bush (*Buddleia davidii*), and the Tardiva peegee hydrangea (*Hydrangea paniculata* 'Tardiva') combine beautifully in this West Chop garden.

▶ Two Vineyard favorites, lavender and hydrangeas, bloom side by side on this sunny slope.

▲ Designed by Jeff Verner, this flowerbed delights its owners, Robert and Liz Gardiner, as well as the passersby who can see it from the street.

◄ A simple formal garden and arbor create a cool looking summer space in Sara Jane Sylvia's garden.

mixed together. Instead of borders planted only with perennials, or foundation plantings that contain just shrubs, island gardens often combine many types of plants. Blending all types of plants produces landscapes filled with color and texture throughout the season, and in July and August the mix is especially colorful and striking.

Leaving It to the Pros

Many who own property on the Vineyard aren't on the island in June, when it's time to plant, or in October, when their gardens are ready for fall cleanup. Some don't have an affinity for gardening or the time to tend a landscape, so hiring a professional gardener is a necessity. As the Vineyard has gained in popularity and population over the last twenty-some years, the desire for professionally planted gardens has grown considerably, and the business of designing and maintaining lawns and gardens has expanded proportionally.

Michael Donaroma, owner of Donaroma's Nursery in Edgartown, says that the growth on the island was certainly

▲ The landscape crew from Donaroma's keeps the mandevilla vine and other annuals blooming in Rosalie Shane's garden.

◄ Rosalie Shane's Edgartown flower garden is filled with a rainbow of perennials. This bed is planted by Donaroma's Nursery.

▲ Jeff Verner designed a beautiful flower garden to surround Jennifer and Michael Phillips's patio and pool.

◄ 'Annabelle' hydrangeas, a crape myrtle, and a magnolia tree are a few of the plants that Jeff Verner used to create an entry garden for this home in Oak Bluffs.

◀▲The Phillipses' garden wraps around three sides of the swimming pool. Knowing that bright colors often show best in the hot summer sun, Jeff Verner planted two varieties of perennial *Rudbeckia* along with the pink cosmos and other annuals.

▲ The rose hips on *Rosa rugosa* are as ornamental as the flowers that grow behind them. In several places in this garden, Jeff Verner planted the lavender-flowering 'Blue Fortune' hyssop (*Agastache foeniculum* X *rugosa* 'Blue Fortune'), which is a long-blooming perennial.

▼ The street side of Donaroma's Nursery is always filled with a beautifully designed feature that's appropriate to the season. Sometimes this old cart is used to hold a display, and other antiques or objects of interest are used as well.

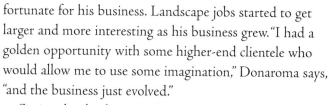

fortunate for his business. Landscape jobs started to get larger and more interesting as his business grew. "I had a golden opportunity with some higher-end clientele who would allow me to use some imagination," Donaroma says, "and the business just evolved."

Saying that his business "just evolved" is a bit of an understatement. With a great deal of hard work and the assistance of talented employees, Donaroma's company has grown over the last thirty years into a full-service garden center that employs around a hundred people during the summer season.

Michael and his wife, Janice, who is a designer and an organizer of several island fund-raisers, say that the scale of the landscaping jobs in the Edgartown area isn't the only area where they've seen changes. "It used to be strictly pastels," Michael remembers, "no red or orange flowers were allowed in Edgartown. But now it's loosened up and there are clients who like the wowie-zowie colors. People are allowed to express their own personality."

Alicia Lesnikowska, who works in gardens throughout the island, has also seen a change. "When we started thirty year ago it was petunias, lobelia, and geraniums," Alicia says. But clients are now interested in unusual plants or a greater mix of species in their containers and flowerbeds.

◄ Alicia Lesnikowska, a professional gardener, was at the campground early on Illumination Day to help Ellen Descheneaux with final garden touches. The gardens surrounding the Victorian cottages are often as colorful as the architecture.

◄▼ Large gardens are made more interesting and intimate when they are divided into smaller spaces, and that's just what Michael Faraca has done at Sweetenwater Farm. He has designed several places where you can see from one area into another.

▼ The pavers that Michael Faraca placed in the Sullivans' herb garden make this garden room more interesting, and they are functional as well. They separate the plants and provide places to stand when picking the herbs.

▶ Michael Faraca, the Avant Gardener, has used annuals to fill beds and containers around the pond at Sweetenwater Farm. Many gardens here are designed around the beautiful garden ornaments that the owners have collected.

▶▶ Abigail Higgins plants and maintains the lovely terraced pool garden at the William Worth Pease House in Edgartown.

Michael Faraca gives Michael Donaroma much of the credit for bringing an increased palette of plants to the island. "I'd say that if there is one person responsible for Edgartown being horticulturally aware, it's Michael Donaroma," he says. Michael Faraca is known as the Avant Gardener, and he keeps a few large properties beautifully planted and maintained through the summer.

Faraca thinks that the structure of Edgartown itself may even play a role in the popularity of certain plants and the desirability of gardens. "Gardening is contagious in Edgartown," he observes, "because the properties are so visible. Neighbors often have a view into the yard next door, and many gardens are visible from the street. People see a plant or a style of garden on their neighbor's property, and it makes them want to do something like it in their yard."

Professional gardeners on the Vineyard often find that their clients use their gardens as an extension of their homes. "I think that the uniqueness is that people *really appreciate* sitting and enjoying their own property," Michael Donaroma says. "A lot of our clients put emphasis on their entertaining—they use the landscape for cocktail parties, charity events, weddings, and large parties."

Janice Donaroma adds that landscapes are important to summer residents on a number of levels. "Aside from entertaining," she explains, "the people who come here often come from cities and they *need color*. Some need all white flowers, some bright colors, and some pastels. When a person puts in a summer garden it fulfills needs that they're not getting in the winter."

As a fine-art painter and a gardener, Rick Hoffman agrees that a beautiful landscape contributes to everyone's sense of well-being. "A garden gives you something that's imponderable," Rick says, "something that our culture often doesn't acknowledge. We all want to be surrounded by

beauty." But the lovely scenes that his customers want are summer landscapes. Rick says that gardens with winter interest have no appeal for the people he gardens for, because they're on the island mainly from July through September.

For the landscape gardener this total focus on two or three months brings a certain amount of pressure. The property owners are outdoors a great deal, and they understandably want their garden to be as flawless as possible. The garden designer needs to take his or her clients' preferences into account, and if a property owner isn't familiar with plants or the peculiarities of Vineyard gardening, a garden installation can be part landscaping and part landscape education.

In addition to being a professional gardener, Abigail Higgins is a garden writer and a source of information about Vineyard plants. Since 2002 she has been writing a garden column for the *Martha's Vineyard Times*, helping keep Vineyard gardeners informed about plants and gardening. Abigail finds that working with her customers can involve garden instruction as well. Part of the professional's job, she says, is to explain the individuality of a given location and how that affects the choice of plants or the garden's style.

"Because I've lived there all my life," Abigail continues, "I have a feel for the island locations. I like to try to make a garden feel as if it belongs and to use plants that look like they've always been there." Higgins also uses earth-friendly

Summer Flowers

Here are a few of the wonderful shrubs, perennials, and annuals that keep July and August in constant bloom.

Shrubs

Annabelle hydrangeas. *Hydrangea arborescens* 'Annabelle' is a stunning shrub with large, white flowers that turn a pale green as summer ends. This hydrangea grows to be about five feet tall and six feet wide, but because it blooms on new growth, it can be pruned back heavily in the late winter or early spring. Plant 'Annabelle' in full or part sun where the soil is well drained but not allowed to go completely dry.

Blue hydrangeas. Commonly called mophead hydrangeas, these shrubs are island favorites for good reason. The shades of blue found in hydrangeas are not common in other flowers, and the size of the blossoms and length of bloom make these one of the most popular plants on the island. 'Nikko Blue' is a widely used variety, but there are many other kinds to choose from as well. Plants should be sited where they can grow to their full height and width because it is impossible to keep them shorter than their natural size.

'Knock Out' rose. One of the best roses to be introduced in the last few years is the 'Knock Out' (*Rosa* 'Radrazz') shrub rose. Highly disease-resistant foliage that's a deep blue-green and bright, deep rose flowers that bloom all summer —what's not to love? 'Knock Out' grows to about 4 feet high and wide. Treat it as you would any rose, and plant it in full sun and well-amended soil.

Peegee hydrangea. When I do consultations, I often recommend *Hydrangea paniculata* 'Grandiflora', commonly called peegee hydrangea. As I describe this plant, the client usually breaks in, saying, "Oh, I *love* that plant!" And well they should. This white-flowering hydrangea begins to bloom in late July or early August, and as the flowers age into September and October, the petals turn pink. This is a bone-hardy shrub that blooms on new growth, so there is no fear about pruning at the wrong time. The peegee can be kept in a shrub form that grows 6 to 8 feet high, or it can be limbed up into a standard or tree form.

The Fairy Rose. If the bright rose pink flowers of the 'Knock Out' rose are too intense for you, try the Fairy. This shrub, at 3 to 4 feet tall and wide, is a good size for combining with annuals and perennials. Clusters of pale pink flowers cover the shrub in June, and the plant will quickly make more if deadheaded. Even without the removal of spent flowers, however, this rose will continue blooming all summer.

Perennials

Agastache 'Blue Fortune'. This perennial is rapidly becoming a classic garden plant, and with good reason. Growing 3 to 4 feet high and blooming from July well into September, 'Blue Fortune' is perfect for many types of landscapes. Like other *Agastaches*, 'Blue Fortune' attracts butterflies, but unlike the similar *Agastache foeniculum*, it does not self-seed around the garden and in every sidewalk crack. 'Blue Fortune' *Agastache* combines well with grasses and *Sedum* 'Autumn Joy', especially in those dry, sunny places where other plants would sulk or die.

Daylilies. There is a daylily for every garden. Tall, short, blooming early or late, fragrant or not, there is a hybrid *Hemerocallis* for everyone. Check tags or descriptions for blooming periods so that there will be daylilies in your garden from June through August, and then stand back and enjoy. Other than feeding liberally with organic fertilizers and cutting down the stalks when flowering is finished, daylilies require very little care.

Hardy hibiscus. Although they may not fit in the tiniest of gardens, *Hibiscus moscheutos* are worth growing just about everywhere else where there is enough sunlight. From the native species that many call rose mallow to the cultivars in a variety of sizes and colors, the hardy hibiscus puts on a late-summer show. Most have flowers that are at least 6 inches around, and many have blossoms that approach the size of dinner plates! Like others in this genus, the rose mallows are late to break dormancy, so don't be concerned if you don't see them emerging until mid-June.

Russian sage. Most perennial tags that say "blooms all summer" lie, but when it comes to *Perovskia atriplicifolia*, the labels are truthful. Russian sage grows to 3 or 4 feet tall, and the wild lavender wands of flowers add color to the garden from July into October. This perennial demands good drainage and full sun, and it tends to grow best when given two or three liberal doses of an organic fertilizer over the season. Russian sage looks best when planted in a group of three or more, and it combines well with grasses, asters, and daylilies.

Annuals

Cosmos 'Bright Lights'. We're all familiar with the lovely pink cosmos that fills beds and borders in the summertime, but people are less well acquainted with the cheerful 'Bright Lights'. This mix of cosmos is smaller both in flower and in height, but the number of blossoms in dazzling orange and gold should be more widely planted. These bold colors catch the summer sun so much better than pastels, and 'Bright Lights' combines beautifully with blue hydrangeas and the other annuals on this list.

Dahlias. Although we often think of dahlias as the queens of September and October, they are beautiful in July and August as well. When started early, these perfectly formed flowers will be in bloom early in the summer and grow taller, and more prolifically, into the fall. Dahlias are a must-have plant for a cutting garden, and they can be integrated into both formal designs and informal plantings. For those who find that their dahlia foliage is attacked by earwigs early in the season, a dusting or two of diatomaceous earth (take care not to inhale the dust) will solve the problem.

Nicotiana langsdorfii. This unique flowering tobacco has smaller flowers than most *Nicotianas* seen in garden centers, but the plant makes up for this with a profusion of lime-green blooms. The cloud of flowers that *Nicotiana langsdorfii* produces combines perfectly with bright or jewel-tone flowers such as dahlias and roses. And for those who want a bit extra, there is a variegated form of this plant that adds white-splashed foliage into the mix. Plant all flowering tobacco in full sun, and then watch for the hummingbirds that they attract.

Scaevola. I'd be willing to nominate this annual from New Zealand as the easiest, most reliable plant you can find for the sunny garden. Many people are used to seeing purple or white *Scaevola aemula* in window boxes or hanging baskets, but it also is perfect for annual and perennial beds or foundation plantings. The common name for this annual is fan flower, but most people just call it *Scaevola*. This annual is sold in pots, not six-packs, and given amended soil and some fertilizer, one plant will fill an area about two feet in diameter.

Sunflowers. If you are afraid of starting plants from seed, it's time to get over it and plant some sunflowers. Although smaller varieties of sunflowers are sold in pots, the larger, more dramatic varieties are not. And there is every reason to put some sunflower seeds in your foundation plantings, your vegetable garden, or your flowerbeds. Sunflowers (*Helianthus annuus*) are cheerful, and the huge yellow flowers look perfect against the blue summer sky. Children love the giant ones, and they grow well in just about any type of soil. Sunflowers are perfect for cutting, and four or five make a dramatic arrangement. When you plant these flowers for cutting, be sure to put in a few extras to leave for the birds. Cover the seeds with a half an inch to an inch of soil in a location where the plants will get as much sun as possible. Keep the soil moist but not constantly wet as the seeds germinate, and then taper off the watering to a deep soaking every five or six days.

Verbena bonariensis. This self-seeding plant is encouraged, although edited, by most gardeners because its form is as useful as the flowers. Clusters of purple flowers top stick-straight stems from July through October, and the blossoms are a butterfly magnet to boot. Although this verbena grows 4 or 5 feet tall, the stems are sturdy and the plant never needs staking. The plant does benefit from having its tips pinched in late June or early July, however, as this will create a fuller, bushier plant.

Zinnias. These are unabashedly happy-looking annuals. Whether planted in groups among other annuals and perennials, or placed in rows in vegetable or cutting gardens, *Zinnia elegans* and its hybrids are to be savored in the summer. Tall varieties such as 'State Fair' and 'Giant Fantasy' produce large flowers on stems that reach 4 feet tall, and the smaller button flowers of 'Cut and Come Again' are popular massed together or in mixed bouquets. For the landscape, the 'Profusion' series of zinnias from Ball Seeds are plants that grow in a neat mound of color. Although these plants are pretty self-sufficient when planted and left to grow, a periodic deadheading does improve their appearance and encourage increased blossoming. Zinnias grow best in full sun. Water these plants deeply but only occasionally: the frequent splashing of water on zinnia foliage may cause leaf-spot fungi or encourage mildew.

▶ Throughout Edgartown the beds of 'Nikko Blue' hydrangeas and 'New Dawn' roses make a winning combination in late June and early July.

▼ Michael Faraca starts these dahlias indoors so that they are in bloom by the Fourth of July.

gardening methods, such as using locally composted wood-chips for mulching the beds, and she explains the advantages of her approach to her readers and customers.

The total attention to summer gardens not only is an opportunity for education about the island environment, but can also be an occasion to view a garden differently. Jeff Verner, a landscape gardener in Edgartown, finds that gardening for two months in the summer is actually a unique way to view the landscape. "Many clients are here only in the summer," Jeff explains, "so the focus is on July and August. . . . It's a different style of gardening because the concentration is so totally on those two months out of twelve. They're not interested in the process of the garden but in seeing perfection during those two months. For us, this often means changing out plants as they go past peak bloom."

Gardening for perfection in a short period can be somewhat like planting a living stage set. In order to be prepared as the season progresses, Verner has greenhouses where he grows some of his own stock. Keeping the plants in peak condition, but not allowing them to be too accelerated in the spring and early summer, can be tricky, but it's necessary in order to ensure that he'll have enough of a particular plant when it's needed.

Michael Donaroma looks at the intense focus on July and August as a positive thing. "You can really go after the

▲ A tall berm protects the plants in this West Chop garden, which is owned by Pearson C. Cummin III and Linda Cummin; it was designed jointly by Linda Cummin and Abigail Higgins. Abigail and her crew maintain the garden, and she says that when the tall *Helianthus* 'Lemon Queen' comes into bloom, this garden is filled with butterflies.

▶ The dark purple foliage of a smoke tree contrasts well with the green leaves of the hydrangeas. In late June the hydrangea blooms emerge with white petals that change to blue as the summer continues.

◀◀ Looking like astilbe flowers on steroids, the white plumes of giant fleece flower (*Persecaria polymorpha*) make a dramatic show in June and early July. Although this plant is tall, it is a very sturdy and trouble-free perennial.

◀ This boxwood-and-lavender knot garden is one of the garden rooms at Sweetenwater Farm. The gardens at Sweetenwater are done by Michael Faraca, the Avant Gardener, and many feature the Sullivans' collection of garden ornaments.

▶ Jeff Verner planted a long flower border of annuals and perennials to line the lawn of this beautiful property in Katama.

◀ Using a mix of annuals and perennials, Michael Faraca has planted a lush flower garden in the backyard at Sweetenwater Farm.

little details," he says, "because it's only two months. You can take the time to tie up every delphinium."

But the concentration on flawlessness can also have environmental consequences if a gardener isn't careful. Alicia Lesnikowska worries that too much water is being used to keep exotic plants alive through the summer months, and Abigail Higgins is concerned about this and other effects on the island environment. "In the last fifteen to twenty years we've seen so many places go to being overlandscaped and overtweaked," she says. "Ecologically it's terrible. Too many substances are being used to produce the look of perfection, and people are cleaning up the *woods*."

At the same time that some professionals worry about cost to wild spaces and resources, others see a new concern about products and practices, and a new ecological awareness on the part of their customers. "Many clients want their properties to be as chemical-free as possible," Michael

Donaroma says. "They're loosening up about the weeds in their lawns, for example."

So island gardeners and landscapers work to provide summer residents with the colorful, inspiring, or restful environments that they come to Martha's Vineyard for, while at the same time being mindful of the island's ecosystems and the overall good of the land. And because the customers notice the visual aspects of the landscape, and aren't necessarily aware of the environmental consequences of the way their gardens are planted, it can be difficult.

Such complexities aside, working to make beautiful island properties also has it rewards. Many would rather work outdoors than be inside. Michael Faraca came to the island to work as a housepainter, but at one point when he was up on a ladder looking into a garden, he thought, "I'd rather be working down there than up here."

Rick Hoffman finds that gardening is a good fit with his

work as an artist. "There's a fine art to gardening," Hoffman explains. "It's turned out to be a wonderful corollary to painting. I get some of my best ideas when I'm weeding. If I'm stumped in my studio, and think, 'Where am I going with this?' I go next door and start weeding, and as I'm working it occurs to me that *this* is what I'm going to do."

For Rick, the focus on July and August in the garden makes some sort of sense. "Perhaps that's truly the peak time of year," Rick muses, "and we're all just following how it's all laid out."

Summer Events

Gardens play a huge role in several annual events on the island. Summer residents often arrive when the roses are blooming and the blue mophead hydrangea flowers are beginning to color. For those who are on the island for the Fourth of July, these flowers seem to perfectly accompany the man-made decorations that adorn many houses and gardens. Paper American flag garlands or cloth buntings

In June you can clearly see the outline of beds in this parterre garden in Edgartown. A parterre garden is usually defined as a level lawn adorned with geometrically shaped flowerbeds. Jeff Verner has planted pink astilbe, light blue *Salvia patens*, and red-foliaged cardinal flower, along with roses and lady's mantle.

Later in the summer 'Blue Fortune' hyssop (*Agastache foeniculum* X *rugosa* 'Blue Fortune') and lime-green flowering tobacco (*Nicotiana langsdorfii*) predominate and soften the straight lines of the garden beds.

▲ Jeff Verner's job is to keep this garden looking full and beautiful through the summer months and, as this photo illustrates, he does it masterfully.

◄◄ Carly Look designed a large planting box filled with annuals for this West Chop home. The snapdragons, *Verbena bonariensis*, petunias, and *Nicotiana sylvestris* that she's planted add color to the deck from late June through September.

◄ Carly Look and her crew keep this West Chop cottage garden looking its best all summer. Like many cottage-style gardens, this one is planted with a combination of shrubs, annuals, perennials, and herbs.

hang from white picket fences in Edgartown, and flags adorn flowerbeds and houses throughout the island.

Later, in August, is the Grand Illumination at the campground in Oak Bluffs. The Victorian gingerbread cottages in and around the campground are as colorful as the flower-filled gardens that surround them, and during Illumination this lively, bright mix of gardens and architecture becomes extravagant with lighting and decorations.

The first Illumination was called Governor's Day because Massachusetts Governor William Claflin was on the island for the event. Organized in 1869 by Erastus P. Carpenter, an off-island businessman, the celebration did not originally take place in the interior of the campground, but was held in Ocean Park. Candlelit paper lanterns were hung from

cottages and trees for the event, and there were fireworks as well.

The occasion was repeated in subsequent years, and it was moved into the Trinity Park area, around the Tabernacle. Many of the Chinese and Japanese lanterns used today have been hung on cottages for scores of Grand Illumination nights, although most cottage owners now use electricity instead of candles to light them. As the lanterns wear out, new ones are purchased and added to the display, but the tradition is that when one of the cottages is sold, the paper lanterns are included in the sale.

Grand Illumination is held on a Wednesday in mid-August, and early evening finds Trinity Park filled with children whirling in excitement and adults strolling around

▲ On the afternoon of Illumination night, Ellen Descheneaux strings paper lanterns all around the perimeter of her property.

◀ During the Grand Illumination the gingerbread cottages in Oak Bluffs are decorated with paper lanterns. After dark a signal is given from the Tabernacle, and the lanterns are lit.

◀◀Michael Faraca points out that his customers will always remember what their gardens looked like at the end of the summer, so he makes sure that he gives his clients a show of color at the end of August. The formal layout of the Conways' parterre garden is softened by the mix of annuals and perennials Faraca has planted in the boxwood hedges.

the campground admiring the decorations. Following a community sing and a concert by the Vineyard Haven Band, a signal is given and the cottages' owners light the lanterns, paper parasols and other decorations. A good-spirited, old-fashioned community atmosphere suffuses the evening, made magical by the fairy-tale lanterns and lighting.

Another August event that is steeped in history and friendship is the annual agricultural fair. This traditional-style county fair runs for four days and is sponsored by the Martha's Vineyard Agricultural Society. Time-honored competitions such as the horse pull and skillet toss are scheduled, and island-grown flowers and vegetables are on display along with other home and farm crafts. Local farmers display animals of all sorts, and there are dog and livestock shows. The fair, held in late August, is a celebration of rural American life *and* summer on the Vineyard.

Swimming through Summer

It is obvious that one of the special aspects of the Vineyard is that you are never far from the ocean. Swimming, fishing, and boating are just a few of the activities that people enjoy on the island. But some people also choose to have access to water just beyond their back doors, so swimming pools have a place in many landscapes, whether or not the ocean is in sight. Gardens surround some of those pools, and there is something very special about swimming in water that's surrounded by flowers, on an island surrounded by water.

▲ Monarch butterflies visit the August-flowering *Asclepias* in a Vineyard summer garden.

▶ Instead of a traditional lawn, this Chilmark house is surrounded by plantings of perennials and grasses. Design by Carly Look.

▼ Zinnias and hardy hibiscus are two plants that are in glorious bloom in August.

▲ Although some gardeners shy away from orange flowers altogether, Michael Faraca knows that brilliant colors will brighten a garden on foggy mornings and stand up to the strong summer sun as well.

▼ Fortunate are those who can spend the summer swimming through this garden. Stonework: Lew French. Gardens: Carly Look.

Most pool gardens are perfect examples of mixed plantings that use shrubs, perennials, annuals, and grasses, so that from June through September there are flowers in bloom. Swimming pools are usually positioned away from trees because of concerns about leaves and other debris falling into the water, so most pool gardens are in sunny locations. This means that those planning these beds have access to the wide range of plants that grow best in full or part sun.

Grasses are commonly planted around pools. They tolerate any sun that is reflected off of the water and hard surfaces that ring the pool, and they soften a landscape with their thin-bladed textures. Swaying in the ocean breezes, grasses add the element of motion to a garden as well, and they evoke the native plantings that are near the shore.

A combination of annuals and perennials guarantees that there will always be flowers in a pool-scape. Perennials such

◄ A pool house built by Lew French and gardens by Carly Look make the area next to the swimming pool look like a scene from a fairytale.

▼ Using large containers, a long flower border, and a flowerbed in front of the pool house, Jeff Verner has created a beautiful landscape around this pool in Edgartown.

▲ Isabelle Shattuck says, "I like to have a splash of white here and there and occasional surprises in the garden." Those splashes of white echo the color of the umbrella, tying the furnishings to the garden.

◄ Isabelle Shattuck says that she wanted to be able to swim in a garden, so she designed a beautiful flower garden that wraps around the pool. With the assistance of Rick Hoffman and his crew, this garden is filled with flowers from June through September.

as blue salvia, iris, and peonies provide color in June while the annuals are still small, and most annuals bloom from early July until hard frost.

Whether these and other summer-flowering plants are placed around a pool, next to a deck, or in mixed borders around a property, their colors and textures truly grace Martha's Vineyard in July and August. Looking at the abundance of Vineyard gardens, whether native plantings, vegetable patches, containers of plants, or flowerbeds, it's easy to agree that on this island the gardeners and residents truly *celebrate* summer.

Containers filled with annuals add to the show of flowers in the Shattucks' pool garden. Although he has planted it mainly with perennials and roses, Rick Hoffman adds a few annuals and says that some of the *Verbena bonariensis* self-seeds, so he never has to replant them.

INDEX

Page numbers given in *italics* refer to illustrations or material contained in their captions.